Restored To Freedom

Restored To Freedom

The Road to Deliverance

From the Enemy's Finest

Nelson L. Schuman

DEDICATION

To all those in the world

who have suffered pain with their parents, adult

relationships, spouses and children. The time is

now to be set free from all enemy torment

and live in love, peace and joy!

ENDORSEMENTS

"This book will guide and direct a believer as they interact with people who struggle with this spirit. Freedom and peace will be the result. The Holy Spirit has led Nelson to expose this dark spirit and give practical steps for deliverance."

Owen Mason – Sr. Pastor, Church Alive,

Lafayette, IN

"I have always wanted to open up a Healing Room in the churches that I pastored but was never able to until God connected me with Nelson. He is truly a man of God that loves hurting people and helping them change from a life of pain to a life of gain. His healing and deliverance anointing is truly miraculous and his heart for hurting people is amazing. He knows how to love like Christ loved the church and walk in His power and authority."

Tim Brown – Sr. Pastor, New Life Assembly of God,

Noblesville, IN

"I got to know Nelson by divine appointment at an overnight canoe trip. We spent all night talking, and soon after he sat under our school of ministry. He has the life experiences to teach, lead, and deliver others from demonic strongholds. I am honored to be a part of how God is using Nelson to set captives and prisoners free. He carries the authority of the believer with true humility."

David Natali – Sr. Pastor, Turning Point Ministries,

Carmel, IN

TESTIMONIES

"I have never read a book that connects all the dots on how a person is affected from the time they first develop the pain from enduring a controlling and rejecting father and/or mother through broken relationships with their spouse(s) and then how to get set free lovingly and gently when realizing what was affecting them for years. It is truly a revelatory book that has saved many lives, marriages and relationships as people are changed from living a life of secret pain to a life of total freedom in Christ. Christ wants his bride to be pure and spotless before Him and this book is doing just that."

"I had suffered much in my life with depression, hopelessness and significant strife in my marriage. I counseled with several pastors but none of them could help me. After learning about spirits that I had affecting me I read some powerful prayers and was totally set free. It literally saved my life and marriage. Thank you for helping me restore my life to freedom."

"I had privately controlled my wife in extreme ways and caused her great pain and actual sickness in her body. I met with Nelson and he explained to me about how when I grew up that my father did not love me unconditionally and how that hurt me severely. He knew exactly what my life used to be like without me even telling him anything. He led me through some prayers and helped me see that the enemy was actually within me causing me to treat my wife horribly. I could finally see that all these years I was the one that was the problem and not my wife. I now have truly changed from a life of pride and domination to a heart that is humble, contrite and loving. Thank you for saving my marriage and life."

"My father rejected and controlled me and my mother never loved me. I had three men that divorced me before my current husband married me. I then immediately started controlling my new husband in extreme ways and abusing him over and over. I blamed him for all my pain and took out all my anger on him while he just took it and loved my children. Then after many years I tried to stop him from ministering and he could no longer take it and separated from me. Then I decided to control him more and lie about him and divorce him. After a lifetime of fear, anger, and strife I finally learned what was wrong – it was me all along and the spirits that were afflicting me. Thank you for opening my eyes to the truth."

"I had been hurt so much by my father and it felt like my heart was broken into a million pieces. Then when I met my husband I treated him very badly and blamed him for everything. I controlled and manipulated him and every counselor we saw could not fix it. Then I finally learned about the spirits that hurt me from this book and read the powerful prayers in it and commanded all spirits to go and was set free. Thank you so much for saving my marriage."

"As a pastor I had never been taught about how these spirits could cause people in my congregation to treat their spouses in such ways and how it would affect my church. I never knew how to deal with people that behaved like this until after reading your book. Now I can finally deal effectively and lovingly with the people that are being controlled by these spirits and the victims of their wrath. This helped me save my church from horrible confusion, strife and destruction. I recommend every pastor to get copies of this and have their members read it because everyone has someone that they know afflicted by these spirits and they do not know how to be free."

ACKNOWLEDGEMENTS

I want to thank Robert Mann for his true friendship, discernment, Godly compassion and wisdom during a challenging yet most rewarding time in my life. You are a giving and selfless man of God. You are truly an amazing man of the Lord that loves others and has a great desire to see people come to the Lord. You have earned the "Grandfather To The World" title. I will never forget you and look forward to reigning with you in Heaven and the New Jerusalem someday.

I want to especially thank all of my family and friends that the Lord has brought into my life who truly love me unconditionally and know my heart to help people with all I am capable of through Christ. You are all awesome and I love you for your support and dedication:

(Aggie, April, Ashley, Austin, Becca, Bill, Bob, Bobby, Brandon, Brian, C, Carrie, Cassia, Cindy, Charles, Chris, Chuck, Crystle, David, Dawn, Deborah, Dianna, Duane, Elaine, Erin, Garry, George, Gina, Hannah, Keith, James, Jan, Jana, Jeanne, Jenny, Jess, Jessica, Joe, John, Jordan, Judy, Julie, Larry, Loren, Luke, Mark, Marshall, Marvin, Megan, Michael, Michelle, Misty, Nick, Nova, Owen, Patti, Patty, Paul, Phil, Priscilla, Randy, Remon, Robia, Ron, Steve, Sue, Taylor, Todd, Trond, Tyler, Tim, and Wendy)

TABLE OF CONTENTS

Introduction

Throughout life we have many choices that we make every day but one choice we do not have a say in is who our parents are. Sometimes we are fortunate and have good, emotionally healthy, stable and unconditionally loving parents. We grow up feeling secure, wanted, comforted and protected. But for many people they grow up with one or sometimes both parents who treated them with love only if they performed exactly as they were told (conditional love). Otherwise their parents might have manipulated them through fear and rejection. They also may have leveraged an unhealthy control over their children through subtle statements and verbal anger outbursts which caused fear to force submission. In the worst cases, some children were actually abused physically and/or sexually. There are a lot of hurting children in homes throughout this fallen world whose hearts have been hurt, scarred and broken. The damage becomes a vicious cycle that if never dealt with causes hurting children to develop into adults who are hopeless, with feelings of confusion, rejection, depression, despair, anger and a desire to take out their pain on their loved ones through control, manipulation and abuse. Some even get to the point of having no desire to live. When these people get married they bring their hurts and pains into the marriage and unfortunately one or both spew their pain onto each other. Strife becomes the norm and sometimes the innocent spouse feels as if they must leave and possibly divorce just to survive – but is that what God wants for the couple? God wants them to be made whole with every past scar healed. Healing brings love and peace with no fear. What if a person is behaving in ways that hurt their spouse and they cannot seem to find that any of their relationships are at peace, due to all the pain of their childhood?

I was amazed when the Lord started to give me revelation and understanding of these sad situations and then revealed to me how to bring about healing and restoration. Many people that He started to bring into my life had either suffered themselves or were married to someone who was wounded by a parent or both. I have spoken to many pastors who have counseled hundreds of married couples where a spouse had been hurt by a father who did not love them unconditionally (or had a mother that did not love them the way they should have). I concluded that this was a generational issue because many of their parents did not have mothers or fathers that loved them the way they should. It broke my heart to see just how many did not have an unconditional loving father and/or mother and are suffering a lifetime filled with strife in their relationships because of it. I was so encouraged when the Lord showed me what needed to occur to get these hurting people completely set free as it was a spiritual issue that was at the root of all their pain and dysfunction. The Holy Spirit began using me to help open the eyes of hurting people to how the pain of their past affected their relationships today. Their lives changed dramatically by reading a few powerful and effective prayers from their heart with many literally saving their marriages. I want to let you know there is hope for your life and marriage to change dramatically. You can be healed and see some very impactful and almost immediate changes in yourself or your loved ones simply by taking authority over the real enemy of this world. Satan wants to steal, kill and destroy you.

John 10:10 NKJV states *"The thief does not come except to steal, and to kill, and to destroy. I have come that they may have life, and that they may have it more abundantly."* Ephesians 6:12 NKJV also points out *"For we do not wrestle against flesh and blood, but against principalities, against powers, against the rulers of the darkness of this age, against spiritual hosts of wickedness in the heavenly places."*

I have seen people go from a life of fear, anger, control, pride, hopelessness, depression and on the verge of divorce to a life of love, joy and peace immediately or soon after praying the prayers that are in this book. This will only work if you truly mean it with a sincere, repentant, humble and contrite heart. So it is up to each one that reads this book. If you or your spouse are truly tired of living a life of misery, blaming everyone else in the world for your pain – and ready for a life full of joy and peace. Read on and let the Holy Spirit open your eyes and shine the light of truth to set all captives free from the past!

Chapter 1

In The Beginning

Think about it....billions of people have come and gone in this world. Some have been fortunate and enjoyed a life full of love, peace and prosperity.....but many have experienced a life full of emptiness, strife, fear, hopelessness, anger and depression. It all starts after they are born into a family with their father and mother. Let's say that when they grew up their father was not around much because he was working a lot. Or when he was home he didn't spend much, if any, time with his children or was the authoritarian with rules and restrictions and behaved very "rough around the edges." He could of been very "religious" without showing unconditional love. Therefore his children never felt very close to him because he was just not involved much in their lives or if he was there he showed little to no true gentleness and unconditional love. He might have been there physically but not emotionally. Perhaps at times he would say things that hurt his children and caused them to not feel loved or even safe around him. Maybe he was more controlling and judgmental than he should have been and did not let them make their own decisions in order to learn from their mistakes. The father may have criticized them constantly which caused them to be unsure of making simple decisions the rest of their lives for fear of his words of correction and wanting his approval. Perhaps he did not want to spend much time around them because he was selfish and this caused his children to suffer feelings of rejection and hurt. What happened to their hearts? Did they feel sad, afraid, and not safe from the man that should have been their protector? They were not able to share their own feelings in their heart, fears or dreams because he would shut them down thus causing their hearts to feel like a knife had just been shoved into it over and over again. He might have ignored, laughed at, or mocked them showing contempt, belittling them or worse - yelled and berated them. They were never good enough and never felt loved because they always had to perform perfectly in his eyes just to receive a little bit of attention trying to "earn the love" of their father.

So why did the father treat them like this? Probably because the father's own father did not truly know how to love, but was harsh, with strict rules and perhaps treated them with verbal and physical abuse. Or perhaps he did not even have a father when he grew up. So it becomes a vicious cycle of pain and hurt being passed on from generation to generation through the blood lines that if never broken will continue to wreak havoc in all the lives of their descendants. Sadly family dysfunction has become representative of our world today.

A young girl or boy who grows up with a father who exhibits some of the behaviors (starting on the next page), will usually be affected negatively, often times for a lifetime, if they never receive healing and restoration in their hearts. The more of the wounding behaviors that one had to endure the stronger the enemy will afflict and hurt them. This will cause them to behave more harshly and hurtful towards others, especially to their own spouse and children and possibly co-workers and church members. Many of these victims cannot see what they are doing to push others away from them with their behavior. Many will suffer greatly and have much pain in their hearts that is so deep and agonizing that they never recover throughout their lifetime and die early deaths full of depression, sadness and despair. Keep in mind there is a continuum of affect that occurs when a father causes their child pain over their youth and formative years. If the father was simply not present much, rather than being extremely abusive, then the child's pain will be in direct proportion and the effects of the enemy on them will be as well. The greater the pain, the greater the negative impact upon them. If they were brought up later by a step-father that was nice to them they often still suffer from the lack of love from their original earthly father the initial years of their life and thereafter. Their heart was never healed from the original pain of their biological father's lack of presence.

Wounding Father Behaviors:

1) The father was not present because either he was working all the time or emotionally not connected - may have left their mother for a time or permanently - bringing on strong feelings of rejection from the child as they may have blamed themselves for the father leaving.
2) The child could never quite be good enough so desperately sought to earn the love of their father. The child had to perform for them perfectly as much as they were able just to receive a little encouragement, if any.
3) Their father behaved more selfishly than selflessly. Although he may have portrayed himself as loving and altruistic to others outside of the family so he would look good to his

friends or the community. Behind closed doors they were harsh and controlling which caused their children to recognize them as an impostor causing them tremendous resentment of their hypocritical father.

4) The father did not show unconditional love very often if ever – if the child did something they did not like, they let their child know about it and possibly made them apologize several times over many months or possibly years – never truly forgiving them and forgetting. They may have reminded the child over and over again later in life never letting them forget of their "failures" in his controlling eyes causing the child to feel tremendous condemnation.

5) His parenting style was harsh, strict and rules-based - not truly caring, loving, gentle, kind or forgiving.

6) Their father was very controlling and did not allow their child to make mistakes without strong correction - may have berated the child multiple times if they did something they didn't like. The child may have had to "walk on eggshells" around their father and or mother.

7) At times the child may have felt like they were living in a military compound as they had to do exactly what they were told without questioning why and felt completely unloved. "Children should be seen and not heard" mentality and if the father made a mistake in discipline he would rarely apologize or never admit it.

8) What the child did was never considered good enough and they received little or no encouragement and almost no words of affirmation were given. The child was basically starving for just a little attention with unconditional love and approval. So the child would strive desperately for attention whether good or bad.

9) In some cases….the father (and possibly mother) really never wanted their child and rejected them over and over and were verbally abusive. The child could have been rejected in the

womb from the very beginning which caused deep pain from before birth. Perhaps the parents did not have much money when they got pregnant with their child or they might have had another child shortly prior to the latest birth or they wanted a boy instead of a girl or vice versa.

10) At the most extreme spectrum the child could have been emotionally abused (yelling, screaming, berating, extreme control) or physically/sexually abused in the very worst cases. The parent(s) completely fractured the child's self-esteem and ability to function.

11) The child's mother could have contributed to the lack of love due to how she was raised accepting it as the norm in her life to be abused by her own father or she felt helpless to stop the abuse because she could have suffered abuse by the child's father had she spoken up.

12) As a double whammy, the child's mother could have treated them harshly and controlling without love due to not being loved from her own father. The result is more pain on top of the lack of love and rejection from their father, essentially increasing their broken heart and creating more pain, pent-up anger and resentment.

Do the above behaviors remind you of your family situation growing up? If so, you are not alone. This is much more common than many know because the child will typically keep it as a secret in hopes that their parent(s) will one day change and ask for their forgiveness for treating them so harshly and love them just a little bit unconditionally. The child is so desperate to be loved that they will endure anything in hopes of getting a "love you" word from their parent(s), even if they know that their actions do not line up with their words.

If you experienced several of these behaviors growing up then the enemy could have gained access to you through your wounded heart, through no fault of your own, because of the painful circumstances you were forced to endure. Unfortunately the enemy is legally permitted to attach himself to the child due to the tremendous pain, anger and bitterness that developed throughout childhood. This is critical to understand because when anger and bitterness take hold in one's life it opens up the door to allow the enemy to walk in and literally take residence. Seven or more of these wounding behaviors could have developed a stronghold of enemy territory that could cause a lifetime of strife with opposite sex close relationships, your spouse and children. If you experienced most of the above mentioned wounds in your youth, you could have developed major pain that if not dealt with through forgiveness and deliverance would cause you to live in significant pain emotionally, spiritually and physically. You may suffer from fear, anxiety, rejection, anger, depression and hopelessness for a lifetime that if not processed and healed by Jesus would lead to torment and devastation. I am truly sorry for all those that have gone through such a painful and unbearable life experience and wish that you never had to endure such trauma.

Women are affected at a higher rate than men when suffering under the above scenarios. If 100 people had been afflicted by the enemy through wounding behaviors of their fathers, you would typically see about 85 women and 15 men that would later develop enemy control. Why? A daughter's heart was made to be treated more tenderly and treasured - to be handled gently with care. A son's heart was designed to be able to withstand more challenging circumstances but, nevertheless, if a father is too overbearing, harsh and abusive then a boy's heart will be hurt just the same and cause major challenges later in life with his relationships. Men were designed by God to protect and provide for their families while women were created to nurture and comfort. When this does not occur, children grow up with tremendous pain in their hearts, minds, and spirits which makes them feel as if they have been stabbed over and over in their hearts and are emotionally bleeding inside until the time they are healed and set free.

23

CHAPTER 2

WHAT HAPPENS NEXT?

So what happens to a child raised under many of these unpleasant circumstances? The child grows up feeling unloved and possibly afraid of their father and most men (and if the mother treated them without love then they could have additional fear and lack of trust of women as well). Because the child does not feel loved, and is in fear of their father, they are not free to share their hopes, dreams or true concerns in an honest way with their parent(s). Their hearts have been broken, crushed and stepped on and they feel no sense of security or protection. Consequently, the child develops feelings of rejection that can affect them the rest of their lives. If anyone says anything to them that they do not agree with, they could be triggered to put up a wall of defense and be offended at the drop of a hat. They will offend others with their negative behaviors continuously in order to protect their own selfish interests so they can survive and thrive at the expense of those around them because they trust no one. They look to themselves first as they feel they cannot depend on anyone else in the world to protect them, including God who their earthly father represented.

This usually will produce deep feelings (and ultimately spirits) of fear, rejection and abandonment which, over time, produces a belief system of extreme fear, anxiety, shame, loneliness and of being unwanted. Ironically this in turn can develop into behaviors of wanting to please people as much as possible and to be a perfectionist in order to earn just a little approval and the kind of love their father never gave them. If they are just "good enough" their father or mother might like them a little bit and tell them they love them – even though it is a conditional love that could be pulled at any point. Some parents have been known to "disown" their children because they did not do exactly what they wanted them to do. Some parents write a child into and out of their will in order to control and manipulate them. Because mistakes triggered their father's or mother's displeasure or anger, the child will try very hard to be "good" and act perfectly according to their parents' desires (which their fathers' and / or mothers' wishes will normally be demanding, unloving and not healthy) in hopes of receiving just a little approval or some token of love from the parent. When the child grows up with the concept that their earthly father (who formed their view of all men, husbands and God) does not want or love them unconditionally, then they are left to protect themselves and always feel alone and in fear, never able to truly trust God to meet their needs and provide security for them. They can never trust their husband even if the husband loved them like Christ. Due to viewing their world through a cloudy lens of fear they are constantly having to control and manipulate the spouse in extreme ways, pushing them further and further away.

This person will feel very insecure, inferior and intimidated and possibly afraid of their father thus developing a view that fathers (and all men in general) only disappoint or hurt them (emotionally and physically). They believe that they have to control all their circumstances at an extreme level to survive because they have no trust in anyone except themselves, and will do everything possible to keep others from seeing who they really are inside. Yet their spouse and children will see and experience all the negative behaviors over and over and over again. Because they do not trust anyone else they usually will not delegate anything significant to anyone because they feel the job or task will not be done correctly. If they do delegate a task to family, the family member will be constantly corrected and it will never be right in their eyes so they will receive verbal harassment. They believe others will let them down and so they must complete the job themselves or it will not get done right. They also have to hide their mistakes because they might receive a word of correction from their spouse or a manager at work which they are not able to bear to receive any practical instructions due to the constant correction and criticism from their own father and possibly mother which brings up reminders of failure and condemnation to them. So they develop the need to try and cover up their negative behaviors which eventually leads to lying because they cannot be honest with having any faults or making mistakes. They believe "If people do not learn that I am doing these negative behaviors then I will not have to receive correction or criticism and can continue to get away with it and no one will find out the truth of who I really am." Unfortunately they are always looking over their shoulder as they must be sure no one finds out about any negative behavior as it would be considered wrong and make them feel bad about themselves again. When people learn who they really are behind closed doors, they will feel horrible about themselves and they cannot take any more criticism since they have endured a lifetime of it from their father and/or mother. Ultimately, they may end up concealing things and of course not wanting their spouse to know

26

what they are up to because they would not be able to get away with some of their behavior if their spouse actually knew all that they were doing. They continue to look over their shoulder and need to make up one lie to cover up another.

It is truly a tormented life of fear, deceit, manipulation and control as the web of lies is spun every day, month, year and possibly a lifetime. So a woman may, for example, lie to their husband about things that they are doing knowing they would not be pleased. They could also feel the need to attack anyone who is in authority over them to try to take control as they do not trust anyone but themselves. They want to show them "I am the boss" before those people disappoint or hurt them again (including their earthly father, husband, their male manager at work, possibly even their pastor, and God the Father).

So what happens when a woman who was hurt from her father attends church? Usually women will initially behave nicely and helpful to their pastor because no one would tolerate anything blatantly controlling. Eventually they may try to manipulate them subtly by saying things such as "you are so anointed and amazing" or "the Lord is really using you – could I pray for you and intercede for you?" They work their way of manipulation slowly through doing favors so they can get the leadership to trust them and will do what they need in order to have the blessing and protection inside of the church. They need to "get in good" with the leadership of the church because they will have preferential treatment and possibly be given more authority within the church to reign over others if they have the blessing of the leadership. They know that if they have the backing of leaders at their church or ministry then they will be able to get what they want with other members of the church/ministry and with their spouse. Often times they will ask to pray for many in the church which causes them to feel good about themselves and cause others to thing they truly are an altruistic godly person who is putting others' needs in front of their own. They seek to create a level of trust from others in the church pretending they are truly concerned

27

for them and want to "intercede" for others hoping for them to feel more dependent upon them. That is how they develop the ability to control and manipulate others by gaining the people's trust that they are such a giving and loving person and know all the answers of how to live a great life. Once the truth is known about them, people would never want to take any advice from them because their lives behind closed doors with their spouse are filled with much strife. Over time they start to move toward more control of those in the church/ministry and other leaders by subtly whispering to them to get them to do what they want. They will often times tell lies about other people and tell the person they are whispering the lies to not say a word about this to anyone. That way they can keep dividing people in the church little by little and no one will be the wiser. They will persist until those in leadership give in and as a last resort, come against them in stronger manipulating ways.

There is no good that will ultimately come from this behavior. Some may try to use the support from their pastors and senior leadership who believe their lies to come against their own spouse if they are losing control of them and then try to leverage a "justifiable" reason for divorce if they are no longer able to get what they want. There would be no grounds for divorce whatsoever and they were the ones that actually abused their loving and Godly spouse which causes the Lord and others that discern the truth to be very grieved. Due to the lies they are able to get the backing of their supportive pastors and leaders to allow this evil and demonic deed to occur. They may even lie and state that their spouses abused them in order to sell their story which is the ultimate slap in the face to their abused victims.

A man with this spirit will typically try to control his wife by not allowing her to make any significant decisions and by not agreeing to any of her opinions and will often times become verbally abusive and extremely controlling and sometimes physically and or sexually abusive, as they will use sex to please themselves. In other words, the husband will dominate his wife and children into

28

submission. The controlling husband or wife may also talk to leaders at their church to plant seeds of lies in order to get their support and trust over their suffering spouse. It is such a hopeless feeling for the spouse of a person that operates in this manner.

If a woman is afflicted by this spirit, she will behave in a very controlling and manipulative way with her husband to make him do everything she wants. Many times she will be intimidating and in the worst cases both verbally and physically violent in order to get her own way, causing her husband to feel emasculated and beaten down and fearful at what she might do next. She often times has a strong desire for sexual gratification herself and will demand it whenever she wants it. She also will control her spouse by limiting him to get her way before she will allow him to receive his healthy sexual needs. This is manipulation at its worst as the husband will feel so controlled that he just wants to give up and walk away from his wife in order to bring peace and normalcy back to his life.

Often times a person afflicted by this spirit has no idea just how overbearing they are to live with due to the cloudy lens of pain and fear through which they are viewing their life and circumstances. They blame their spouse for creating the strife when in reality it was completely their own fault all along and is as one-sided blame as anyone could imagine (although most will not believe that it could be mainly one person's fault). They will defend their behavior and go round and round in circles in various arguments and strife until their spouse is filled with hopelessness and suffers feelings of depression and after years of suffering possibly having thoughts of divorce or even suicide. The victim often times feels like they are going crazy because the controlling spouse will talk like they did nothing wrong and it was their spouse's fault all of the time yet they will take no responsibility for creating the strife in the first place hundreds if not thousands of times. It is also common that the victim spouse could develop some sickness in their body as they grow so hopeless in seeing their spouse never change. The barrage of control and abuse will become worse over time. Some victims of abuse may even develop cancer or suffer heart attacks as the constant verbal abuse and control over a lifetime takes its toll on one's body.

What the child really needed was a father who loved them without condition; a father who demonstrated that they were valuable, loved and protected. They needed a father that would listen to them and let them sit on their laps and be held and given unconditional love and care. However, because the individual was not loved in this way, they developed a coping mechanism of self-protection in the form of unhealthy control and manipulation in order to avoid further pain and harm to their already wounded hearts, minds and spirits. They now have a tremendous fear of loss and an overwhelming need to control at an extreme level. A consequence of this lack of unconditional love and subsequent lack of trust in authority figures is the development of unforgiveness, bitterness, fear, anger, lying and rage in the person as they grow older. Unfortunately all of these bad memories have never been resolved successfully nor healed by Jesus through true forgiveness. The anger from their past states that *all trust is gone, be suspicious of everyone who even resembles those from the past (i.e. a man)* and the new motto is *deactivate possible attackers before they can hurt me again* from which the person can actually develop a feeling of vindication when calculating who they want to hurt next. You can see it in their eyes as the spirit inside of them causes them to become a different person full of anger and hatred as they want to pay back all the pain that they had to take from their own father onto someone else that represents their father. It is a very controlling, twisted and evil spirit on them as the enemy speaks to them over and over and they will often times know it is the enemy that they are hearing yet do not know how to get it to go from them. In most cases they would rather keep their behavior and lie about their spouse or others in order to protect their reputation in the community and church than to ever repent of their lies and be honest in order to ultimately be totally set free. This is the manifestation of a true spiritual tug of war like none other in this world.

The avenue of counseling has been explored by many couples unsuccessfully due to the controlling spouse not being honest. Private conversations with church and ministry leadership and influential people, spinning their web of lies within the key decision makers of a church/ministry so that when it comes time to engage their spouse in counseling, the pastors or counselors will believe the person who set them up instead of the true victim who was abused their whole marriage or relationship. So then the victim gets abused all over again and one of two things will happen. Either the victim has had enough and will separate and may ultimately divorce the one that they tried desperately to love but could no longer take the control, manipulation and deceit or the dominating spouse will choose to keep their lies and false reputation and make up more lies so they can justify a sinful divorce with their spouse often times telling people that they were the ones abused to turn it all around on their victim. So then no one knows who is telling the truth and the people in the middle, who love both of them, are greatly saddened, confused and distressed. Instead of the abuser changing and becoming humble and contrite they become more indignant, prideful and dominating waiting for their next victim to devour.

It is a very depressing state of affairs indeed that grieves the Holy Spirit and all those that love both of the people because no one knows who is telling the truth unless they have a strong gift of discernment and hear from the Holy Spirit. Sometimes the leadership of the church may suffer from the same spirit so they will actually protect the controlling spouse and force the true victim out of the church who will then feel even more abused and hopeless. The like spirits in both the controlling spouse and the church leadership will team up against the true victim. The true victim spouse may ultimately decide to move as far away from their spouse as possible to never see them again and not deal with all those that believed their lies and then give them over to the enemy. It is a very sad situation for the true victim who is often times a very meek, virtuous and Godly person who was "framed" by the spouse that was abusing them for their entire marriage.

There is no worse feeling in this world then to have those that are in leadership at your own church that you love, believe lies about you that were told by your own controlling spouse that you loved yet have been abused by for so many years. In trying to protect them and keep their abuse secret you hold out hope that they would eventually change and be honest and healed through your unconditional love. Loving someone like Christ loved the church is truly something that can be extremely hard to do when someone is being afflicted by the enemy. God sees and knows all and will eventually bring the truth to light whether it takes a few months or even years – trust in the Lord.

Ephesians 5:11-13 NKJV *"¹¹And have no fellowship with the unfruitful works of darkness, but rather expose them. ¹²For it is shameful even to speak of those things which are done by them in secret. ¹³But all things that are exposed are made manifest by the light, for whatever makes manifest is light."*

If a person is not healed from their broken heart, they will commonly go through a life of several strife-filled relationships always blaming their spouses and never taking ownership for their own bad behavior and actions. When they speak with a counselor they will lie and never be honest with how they were the cause of the majority of the strife. Then when they eventually marry, the marriage becomes nothing but conflict and arguments, with much suffering and misery which will lead to separation and often times end in divorce as the victim gives up hope of ever seeing true change and repentance from their abusive and controlling spouse. They may experience multiple divorces over time, always telling everyone that knows them that it was the other person's fault and if the controller is a woman then she will be especially skilled at playing the part of an "abused wife" and victim going to great lengths to prey upon other people to gain support and protect themselves while her spouse feels helpless and frustrated because no one believes him and the truth because after all "how can a woman abuse you as you are a bigger, strong man" as one male pastor ignorantly said to an abused husband.

Joyce Meyer once stated that a woman came up to her at one of her conferences and told her that she had been divorced 4 times and was lamenting to her that she just could not find a good man like Joyce's husband Dave to which Joyce responded "Lady – who is the common denominator in all these divorces – maybe you need to look in the mirror at yourself for once." Don't you just love the honesty with which Joyce lays it out! God knows the truth and has seen everything and eventually the truth will come out as the fruit of each person becomes evident to all. It is time to be honest and be truly set free and pure before the Lord.

Typical counseling sessions with well-meaning but poorly equipped pastors or counselors do not work because the controlling spirit in the person knows exactly what to say and how to say it to lie undetected to their counselors. Sadly it is a waste of time and money because the controlling person will never be honest thus they will never be able to be set free and changed. Their victim will feel like giving up because their controlling spouse acts like they are concerned and they say all the right things in front of the counselor such as that they "really want the marriage to improve" yet when they are behind closed doors they return back to the control, manipulation and deceitful behavior of their past. It is like they are wearing a mask when out in public and are acting on a stage like they are loving, innocent and pure as the wind driven snow but once they have their victim alone - the mask comes off and you see the dark side of what is controlling them inside and it is not pretty. Because they are looking through cloudy lenses, the truth becomes distorted and their inability to accept correction causes them to blame their spouse for everything instead of taking the responsibility for their behavior that is ungodly.

Sadly the general lack of protection and nurturing love experienced by the child has now produced an adult who is very, very hard to live with and almost impossible to love. As a result, the victim spouse will ultimately move out in order to live in more peace (or they may make the controlling person move out of their home if they can) and then the victim waits for their spouse to become more humble and take ownership for their abusive behavior. Change rarely happens because they will never admit to fault and the typical counselors cannot discern who is telling the truth so they get to keep their lies. The controlling spouse will blame their innocent spouse and may leave or divorce them to keep control when the victim did nothing to deserve it other than enduring a lot of extreme strife and pain and concealing the abuse. Eventually, if this is not dealt with, the dominating person will probably get remarried but will then continue their domination of the new victim and another divorce will ensue until they eventually have had multiple divorces and usually become more and more controlling of their future victims as the spirit gains strength over time. You may also see other siblings of the controlling spouse having multiple failed marriages and relationships as well as they will have been hurt by the same father and/or mother and carry the same behaviors of control, manipulation, anger and abuse.

Often times if the abusive spouse is a woman then she will develop sickness and possibly die early due to depression, hopelessness, oppression, loneliness and usually some kind of strong physical pains and possibly receive a disease which will become more prevalent the older they are. If the wife is married to an abusive and controlling husband then usually the victim wife will also suffer from debilitating diseases and many have developed cancer and die in their 50's. It is a very sad and depressing life that they lead and we should feel compassion for the person yet anger towards the controlling spirits that are very wicked within them.

It is a challenge at knowing how to help a person with these spirits and issues because they usually have a desire to truly want to help people deep down inside but unfortunately they become something evil when no one else is looking and the victim suffers greatly in their presence. Truly a "Jekyll and Hyde" type personality that causes a spouse to feel hopeless and depressed and just wanting to run away in order to finally live in a quiet state of peace. The victim feels like they are truly going crazy because they never see improvement from them as their desire for complete control and domination is never satisfied and they always want more. The victim feels like a puppet controlled by an evil master that can do whatever they want to make them do. So there are truly two victims in this scenario, the person who is causing the control and abuse as they are acting out in pain from their childhood – and the spouse that is taking the abuse from them over and over again hundreds and thousands of times. It is very sad and needs to be dealt with effectively because nothing good will ever come of this until the controlling person is truly set free from the enemy. Most pastors and counselors have no idea how to get them totally free because they have never been trained on dealing with these dark spirits that are afflicting the person. Until now – uncovering the true root of the problem is why this book was written! Please understand there is no condemnation for the person who is controlling their spouse – only love, compassion, forgiveness and a desire to help them understand what happened to them. Now we must learn how to become totally free in the Lord. What a beautiful thing it can be!

Chapter 3

Behavior Traits

So what are the common behaviors that people who have endured this type of life in youth exhibit towards their spouse, children or others in the work place? Below is a list of some common traits and, if one is truly honest (and that is the key to this book that the one reading it must be totally honest with themselves), they will probably identify with some or many of them. The more of the pain that they have endured in their life from a father that was overly controlling, rejecting, and hurtful or a mother that was void of unconditional love the more of the behaviors they will exhibit. The more behavior traits that they exhibit the stronger the enemy spirit's control of them will be and the harder it will be for them to admit they may have an underlying issue and the more challenging it will be for them to get free from the unhealthy control of the enemy. There is a continuum and some may only exhibit a few of the behaviors, thus the spirit is not as strong upon them although it could still be present and active. If they exhibit many or most of these traits listed below in their lives then they most likely have the enemy spirit operating with a strong control over their mind in a very dominant way and will tend to be very difficult to become freed. It will be a real challenge to admit anything is impure or ungodly about themselves (and often times they will receive many conflicting and tormenting thoughts from the enemy throughout the day and exhibit a lot of fear and anxiety).

Behavior Traits:

1) They are usually charismatic in personality and very determined to get work and ministry projects completed no matter what stands in their way. They are natural born leaders that are driven to succeed and accomplish goals at all costs. If someone tries to steer them off course they will not be persuaded and will remove all obstacles from their path in order to complete the plan.

2) Will see significant energy bursts yet also feel lethargic at times. When in solitude at the end of the day they feel exhausted and depressed due to all the tormenting thoughts from the enemy. Friends would view them as fun to be around as they are usually full of energy but once they are back home behind closed doors and alone they will feel tired and depleted when their restricted conscience (aka the true Holy Spirit) whispers to them the truth.

3) Likes to be the center of attention and often times the life of the party – so when they come into a room full of people they love people to gravitate towards them and they are very much a people person and dynamic in personality and are very

skilled at playing the emotions of anyone to get them to do what they want.

4) Strong desire to be in control of everything (because of the feelings of rejection and control from their father thus the tendency is to replicate the same behavior with others). They want their way and they will do anything to manipulate to get it. Will do anything to be able to take control of situations every day, week, month, year and a lifetime which can be suffocating for their spouse and children or other victim.

5) They endure a high level of fear, anxiety and restlessness and they typically do not sleep soundly through the night (can even suffer from nightmares) which they try to cover up as best they can around other people but cannot suppress around their spouse and/or children. Often fall asleep when trying to read the Word or listen to someone preaching or speaking about the Bible or spiritual things. They simply do not live a life of peace and those around them may like the energy, excitement and charisma that they offer but will often times need to get away from them in order to feel peace.

6) They hear a voice inside their head that tells them things that cause them fear and anxiety. Often times the voice will cause them to hear things that are not pure, loving or sweet but instead they hear things that tell them to behave selfishly and controlling which cause division and strife between them and their spouse, children or co-workers and church members. This is the voice of the enemy and sometimes the person will know it is the enemy but often times will not be able to make the distinction between hearing the Holy Spirit and hearing the enemy. A constant state of torment is common.

7) Very insecure in oneself (they will try to compensate by acting like they are self-assured and knowledgeable on everything) so they like to tell people things they have accomplished and may want to one up others stories of life making themselves look better and perfect in order to make them feel better about themselves but it is fairly simple to pick up on if you are around them much. Sometimes will lie about their father's true behavior in order to act like they had a great father because the pain of revealing the truth of how they were hurt causes them even more pain.

8) Often will make statements to guilt their victims in order to cause others to do what they want. Very manipulative and usually their victims can feel that something is definitely wrong and they are being controlled. Spouses will know this feeling as it will be commonly spoken to them on a regular basis many times over and over.

9) Significant strife with their spouse that will typically be least in the morning but much more prevalent throughout the day and strongest in the evening. They will usually state that all the strife is their spouses' fault when in reality it is because of the words they say that start the arguments and continues as they do not take responsibility for it because their view of reality is not accurate and they are behaving like their father / mother treated them.

10) Talks incessantly and dominantly – usually a strong Type A personality and normally does not like to lose at any discussion or difference of opinion or even sporting event (can be very competitive). They will talk and dominate all conversations and it becomes tiring if you ever engage in a discussion with them as they can go on for hours and hours

and you feel like you are in a lecture hall listening to the teacher and you are the student.

11) Talks in much confusion especially if confronted with a question about something that they know they have lied about or want to keep hidden. One of their sly ways to slip away once confronted, is to try to confuse their victim by changing the subject multiple times in just a few minutes. Confusion keeps them "undiscovered" and unexposed. Therefore, it is impossible to converse in logic. If confronted in an email or text they could write for pages dealing with all sorts of other situations than the one you are confronting them with. The context would be so vague that no one would understand heads or tails what was just stated. If it is in conversation they would simply talk nonsense to confuse their victim, never responding to the initial question. In this situation, one has to repeat the question and ask them only to respond to that question but usually they never will.

12) Fearful – they may act like they have faith in God but you simply cannot have faith while being in a constant state of fear. Very worried of people learning negative information about them and how they have behaved in the past or finding out their lies or failed relationships or multiple failed marriages – very suspicious of others honest intentions. Always looking over their shoulder. Those that know them can often feel the fear and anxiety because it is so evident.

13) Dominates relationships – women will usually come across as a drill sergeant and masculine to their husbands instead of soft, loving or supportive and their husbands will feel emasculated and be forced to abdicate all God desired leadership of the family. Hopelessness is evident in them as each week and month that goes by brings more defeat. Men

that are afflicted by this controlling spirit will so dominate their spouse that you can see the look of defeat and deep sadness on their wive's faces and they feel like barely functioning zombies usually suffering from depression and other physical pains and diseases that never get healed and can bring on early death.

14) Always believing their way is right and thus they will often get in a tug of war with their spouse over many minuscule decisions. They want to get their way so much that their spouse will commonly just let them win over and over as it minimizes on power struggles or strife and arguing that could last for hours.

15) Unhealthy jealousy due to insecurity – do not want their spouse talking to someone of the opposite sex or mentioning someone of the opposite sex in conversation to them or if their spouse was married previously to even talk about them at all in a positive light. Very suspicious and may say that their spouse is having an improper relationship with someone when there is nothing unhealthy or wrong about their spouse's opposite sex relationships at all. Thus they manipulate their spouse into having no opposite sex relationships at all.

16) Will eventually come against their spouse especially if the spouse has a strong desire for ministry to try to limit them or even shut them down from operating in the Lord's gifting – perhaps saying that they need to "concentrate on their marriage" issues with them instead of doing what the Lord has called them to do. Or may tell their spouse that "you should not be giving words from the Lord to people of the opposite sex because it is not right."

17) If they are a woman they may touch the arms or shoulders of a man often that they are talking to as they try to subtly "seduce" him with her "femininity" so he will be on their side if they ever need him in the future to side with her or they can manipulate them to do what they want to accomplish. Most men are easy to be played. Some women are genuinely loving in that way so it is important to discern what is healthy and what is over the top.

18) Desire to know every detail and piece of unknown information possible so they can control the outcome of a situation and get what they want. Commonly try to find out inside information about people so they can leverage it to their benefit later as they are very adept at manipulation.

19) Constantly trying to connect with people of position and power to leverage themselves into a stronger position. Usually will try to develop a good relationship with the senior pastor of a church/ministry or others close to the top leadership such as the pastor's daughter or son that have decision making power or can influence someone that does so that they can wield control over others or their hapless spouse in the future.

20) Gift giving – used as a form of manipulation which makes you feel obligated to him/her. Women will often give gifts more than men that are afflicted. Many will give jewelry or other items that they know other women would want in order to "buy" their allegiance in the future.

21) Hides information so they are always one step ahead of others. Secretive and protective to know more than others. May look at spouse's or others phones to try to read private texts or emails in order to know what is being communicated

as their spouse may reach out for true help or support from others and they want to know what is going on at all times. Often times will lie to their spouses in order to get them to stop communicating with other counselors or healthy support of people to control them by making up things about them in order to get them to no longer talk with them.

22) Manipulative over others (especially spouses) – often times very obvious but sometimes very subtly and hard to perceive. They will never give up as they are tenacious at getting what they want and will wear you down until you give up and give them what they want.   They will do this when having discussions with people.

23) Lies very convincingly so that others do not perceive although their spouse can usually tell (very good at acting nice and sweet to others while behaving poorly to their spouse and/or children as they can flip a switch any time it will benefit them). Most people do not want to believe that they are being lied to which makes it even easier for their lies to proliferate. Women can play the victim role very well as most men will fall for their lying words as they can act so innocent and in need of a Prince Charming to help protect them.   Extremely good actresses and actors – Academy Award level.

24) Speak very hurtful words to provoke their victims which will start an argument and then later blame their victims for the strife. Also vengeful if anyone comes against them and exposes their behavior or lies. No one will be more vindictive and looking for payback if you stand in their way and try to expose their evil deeds.

25) Is insubordinate and manipulative – especially if they are a wife married to their husband – saying things like "we need to be one in spirit in this decision" which actually means "you need to do what I want or else you will not have peace with me." Is really impossible to be on the same page with on most any significant decision as they will want their own way constantly and will usually not be the same decision as their spouse would make.

26) Spiritualizes everything and will often know Bible scriptures very well so they can twist them to their own way of controlling their spouse or others. "The Bible says you are to provide a spiritual cover over me" which they twist so that you "do not tell anyone about my extreme control and abuse of you – keep it a secret and protect me so I can continue with my abuse of you." Masters at manipulating scriptures to their advantage causing spouses to feel hopeless.

27) Uses information known only by him/her to their advantage as leverage for power and more control. Often times will talk on the phone to various people or counselors and not allow their spouse or others to hear what they are saying because they are lying in order to gain support from the counselors. May turn on a fan in their room when they are talking so their spouse cannot hear the lies that they are speaking or lock themselves in a closet or walk out to a garage or down the street out of earshot.

28) Very critical and judgmental of others and self-righteous of own behavior. Think that their way of doing things is perfect and everyone else in the world is wrong or sinful. Thinks and behaves much like a modern day Pharisee. Will often brag about their frequent fasts in order to make themselves look good and pious.

29) Hears the voice of the enemy often which drives them to do things that are not Godly, loving or honorable. Thinks at times they are hearing from the Lord when it is the enemy's voice. At times they do hear from the Lord but it is a constant battle for their mind between the enemy and the Lord and more often than not they are hearing the voice of the enemy.

30) Ignores people that are not considered valuable to them at church or in public. If they serve no purpose to them in giving them more power then why spend any time befriending them or spending any time with them. May have cliques at church/ministry that they congregate to and do not truly love all people like Christ has called them to. Will not usually partner with a person that is stronger spiritually than them as they want to be able to control everyone.

31) Will not take responsibility for negative words spoken to their spouse (usually blames spouse for strife even though they started 95% of the arguments with their mean, harsh and condemning words and tone from the enemy). Pushes those away from them in relationships that truly love them but eventually their spouse cannot live with the behavior anymore. Often times do not even know that they are blaming other people for their own issues as it becomes so normal for them.

32) Typically suffers from narcissistic behavior with spouse but appears very altruistically around others especially in the church. If you knew them from church you would often think they are the nicest person ever as they often go out of their way to help people so it is hard to discern who they really are behind closed doors.

33) Large ego and very prideful and arrogant. Rather than seeing themselves as humble, committed servants in God's affairs who at one time volunteered willingly to serve Him, they see themselves as chief executive officers of a large ministry or organization. Their attitude frustrates the people around them. They boss people around, running the spiritual affairs like a business rather than the Kingdom of God. To say the least there is a great need of dying to one's ego and humility that is needed.

34) Sometimes will have a strong sexual appetite and controlling of spouse through sex (either "give it to me when and how I want it" or withholding from spouse to manipulate to get their way) and impure thoughts can come in frequently. Can desire role playing and may need to fantasize. There is minimal intimacy when it comes to sex and does not feel pure and wholesome the way God intended. Uses sex as a tool to accomplish what they want. If sexual desires do not get met then they will find a way to bring themselves release.

35) False humility is very common. They will appear to be very humble in front of others at church and around town but when behind closed doors or in their car they will say things to their spouse and children that are very haughty and proud.

36) Behavior can be very emotionally unstable from high highs to low lows and could be labeled "bipolar", multiple personality disorder and in the more extreme cases even insane in their behavior by their victims. It is never a dull moment with them because they are all over the chart although it becomes quite tiring and exhaustive for their spouse and children.

37) Sometimes can be so angry that they will take on a very scary looking face and make sounds that are intimidating and resemble demonic manifestations (i.e. growling, raising voice, fierceness, eyes of pure hate, etc). They know that by appearing ferocious that they can scare their victims into submission. It wears out their victims seeing them turn a rare peaceful night into a night of terror once again.

38) Extremely controlling of their spouse, children and in some cases even abusive and will often times not have any remorse whatsoever for what they did. May not allow spouse to spend time with certain healthy people or talk/text to them and many other controlling ways. Has limited to no Holy Spirit conviction over controlling behavior.

39) At the worst end of the spectrum if they do not get their way they could throw things such as pens, cell phones, water glasses, knives, break things, try to break down doors where their spouse is hiding from them, verbally berate their spouse in their home and even in bed for hours as the spouse is trying to sleep, threaten to divorce over and over, behave crazy and out of control including chasing their spouse in their house, hotels, making their spouse wait on them for hours in public before they are ready to get in the car to leave. Also could stand behind their spouse's vehicle in their garage so they cannot back up and leave to get away from them and if their spouse runs out of the house they will want to chase them down. In a nutshell they behave in an extreme controlling and intimidating manner knowing that if they can get their spouse to submit they will always get their way. It is a life full of complete misery in every way imaginable for their victim.

40) They can become physically abusive, grabbing arms to force someone to do what they want, shoving their spouse down, even throwing punches, have no problems doing it and will lie to the police or a judge and blame their victim for what they have done to them. They have almost no Holy Spirit consciousness or conviction about them, void of all that is pure and holy especially behind closed doors with their spouse and children.

CHAPTER 4

PHYSICAL TRAITS

There will often times be some physical afflictions on the controlling person that is being tormented by these enemy spirits that prayer may temporarily bring minor relief from but never seems to be able to get the person completely set free....because the tormenting spirit will not allow them to be healed since they have a right to co-exist in the body. Also if you are a woman whose husband has the controlling spirit then you will usually also suffer from physical infirmities and some could be debilitating and deadly as the verbal assaults take a toll on your body, mind and spirit. Therefore the person will become frustrated by not being totally delivered from the pain in their body. Some of the common physical pains in one's body include:

1) Neck pain and tightness with possible restrictions in movement of head from side to side.

2) Tension in the face or eyes. You can see the anxiety and fear and anger in their eyes.

3) Shoulder and back tightness or pain that never seems to go away even after prayer. May have to go to the chiropractor a lot to get adjusted to try to ease the pain and be on painkiller medication.

4) Feeling tenseness in their body, very anxious – never feeling at peace as they always have to make sure that no one finds out the real truth about their behavior and that they remember what lies they have told other people to keep their stories consistent and to keep from being uncovered.

5) Insomnia. Lack of sound sleep so will rarely receive a full night's sleep. May have nightmares that involve someone being hurt.

6) Usually have several physical infirmities in the body from which they cannot receive any healing from even from anointed people – may get temporary ease of pain but it always comes back because the enemy's spirit is still present.

7) Eventually could lead to debilitating diseases especially if the person has been given many chances to renounce the spirit afflicting them once they are aware of it but refuse to admit they could have it.

8) If you are a man being afflicted by the controlling spirit then your wife will often times suffer from poor health and may be deeply depressed, hopeless and could develop many physical afflictions such as fibromyalgia, allergic to various foods and cancer as well as early death.

9) Will often times be in good shape physically because are always on the go but rarely have time to just relax having to keep one step ahead of those that may become aware of their deception and lies.

10) Often times have fear of eating certain foods and how it could affect them. Worried if they do not eat what they consider to be perfect then will have issues. The enemy torments them at many stages of their lives as they become a slave to him.

The older the person, the stronger the likelihood that the person will have a significant physical ailment and/or disease due to the tormenting spirit having had control of the person for so long and ultimately wanting to kill them before they get set free from the enemy and operate freely in doing the Lord's work and minister unencumbered.

There are also common traits that a person's family members might have experienced both immediate and in their ancestral and children's lives. That is because the spirit that is afflicting them will have started way before the person was ever born and will come down the blood line generation after generation until it is finally recognized and broken off. Just think about how many sins your ancestors on both sides of your parents have given enemy spirits access to everyone on down the line. Exodus 34:6-7 "[6] And the Lord passed before him and proclaimed, "The Lord, the Lord God, merciful and gracious, longsuffering, and abounding in goodness and truth, [7]keeping mercy for thousands, forgiving iniquity and transgression and sin, by no means clearing *the guilty,* visiting the iniquity of the fathers upon the children and the children's children to the third and the fourth generation." Also Deuteronomy 5:8-10 "[8] 'You shall not make for yourself a carved image—any likeness *of anything* that *is* in heaven above, or that *is* in the earth beneath, or that *is* in the water under the earth; [9] you shall not bow down to them nor serve them. For I, the Lord your God, *am* a jealous God, visiting the iniquity of the fathers upon the children to the third and fourth *generations* of those who hate Me, [10] but showing mercy to thousands, to those who love Me and keep My commandments."

That is why a doctor will ask you what diseases your parents and grandparents have had because you will most likely have the same afflictions that they did due to the spirits having a right to come down the bloodline from generation to generation. Until those sins and curses are broken and revoked you will be living under them your entire life and be controlled by them and never be able to truly enjoy the life that God wanted and planned for you. So think back through your ancestors right now and write down some of the common areas of infirmities that your family members have endured. This will be a way that you will learn if there are generational spirits that have come down through your blood lines that are affecting you and possibly your own descendants.

Some of these afflictions include the following:

1) Lack of sleep / Insomnia
2) Depression
3) Early death of a family member (could also include suicide)
4) Strong family conflict (lack of unconditional love) to the point that some of the family members may not even be speaking to each other or worse may even take a family member to court
5) Very strong unhealthy sexual appetite
6) Pornography addiction

7) Senility
8) Homosexuality or Lesbian behaviors (women behave more masculine and dominating)
9) Fibro Myalgia
10) Cancer
11) Infertility
12) Diabetes
13) Heart problems
14) Schizophrenia, Multiple Personalities, Insanity
15) Divorce
16) Male or Female domination
17) Incest
18) Curse of Loss of Children
19) Loss of Marriage Partner(s)
20) Loneliness and Desolation
21) Witchcraft /Declaring curses
22) Persecution
23) Being deceitful (not being able to be trusted)
24) Alcoholism
25) Unhealthy addiction to sex / fantasy / role playing

The greater the number of the above afflictions that you have seen in your family and ancestors the more likely that the spirits have been afflicting you and them for a long time and are stronger in their control and need to be broken off. It is truly a dysfunctional situation that will cause family members to feel depressed and hopeless of believing their families will be able to be set free and delivered. It could begin with you after you have read this book if you are willing and agreeable to break the curses that have been on your family and turn what the enemy meant for evil to good.

Chapter 5

What Has Been Tormenting Me?

There are many enemy spirits and some have names that we can identify. What has been harassing a person for years and often times a lifetime since as early as their teens? Why do they behave the way they do? Why can they not live a peace filled, gentle and loving life? Why are they unable to enjoy a loving relationship with their spouse and children even after spending months, years or a lifetime in counseling/therapy? It is a spirit that exhibits much control, manipulation and causes a person to easily lie and drives them to dominate more than any other spirit. It especially attacks those that the Lord has a strong calling on and who could become greatly anointed once completely set free from all the oppressing spirits. Many will become extremely anointed especially that have endured the worst conditions as a child as the enemy wanted to destroy and control, never allowing its victim to become set free and know what has been haunting them for a lifetime.

How does this spirit gain entry into a person? Through the years of pain, rejection, control, anger and possible abuse from the person's father (and sometimes mother) this extreme hurt opens a door to the enemy to come in and have a right to afflict them for the rest of their life until they recognize it and later command the spirits to go. They essentially become like the evil spirit as it takes over their minds instead of who they really are in Christ as the anger, pride, control, manipulation, and deceit spirits are the behaviors that become them. They are usually able to control their actions so that many times only their spouse or children see the dark side of them because they have no place to hide from its wrath. They want to take out all their pain on someone so they usually select the person(s) that represent the person that gave them the most pain. They can also behave that way to a select few that stand in their way at church or in ministry. It is a sad state of affairs for the tormented person and even more so for their spouse who endures the brunt of that spirit every day behind closed doors (and their children and potentially others in their lives). It is as if they are wearing a mask in front of those in the church/ministry as they try to act like they love, are kind and caring while the spirit inside them wants nothing more than to destroy God's anointed people in an undetectable way. Again remember that if you were not hurt as strongly by your father (and mother) then you may just have a small effect of the spirit upon you whereas if you were greatly hurt by both parents then you could have the full force of this spirit operating in your life which will explain all of the relationships that have failed over your lifetime. What is the spirit that encompasses all of these behaviors and treats their loved ones with such fierce control?

It is called the Jezebel spirit – which is the spirit that comes against an anointed person (especially those that flow in the prophetic gifting) and is the most difficult spirit from which to become freed. Why is Jezebel so tightly bound to its victim? The Jezebel afflicted person is the only one that has the power to command the spirit to go once and for all from their own life since they have a free will to choose if they want to keep it or not. So, if you are being attacked by Jezebel, count it as a badge of honor. You could be a very anointed person that the enemy wants to keep afflicted so that you cannot be totally free to operate in the extreme level of anointing that the Lord has called you to. You are destined to help others become free as well. Jezebel means the un-husbanded (or un-wifed if you are a man that has it) and is a counterfeit Holy Spirit - meaning that you will act like you are loving and kind and being directed by the Lord most of the time but instead of being pure and Godly you behave contrary to the Holy Spirit. Jezebel will attack behind closed doors with your spouse and children or co-workers and will usually be quite active within your church/ministry as the spirit wants power, control and recognition and pushes for connection with leadership, pastors and key influencers, trying to work their way into acquiring more power and prestige. Jezebel comes against the true Holy Spirit operating in others' lives. If married to a gifted prophetic spouse who may be operating in the Spirit of Elijah, Jezebel will try to limit that spouses' ability to use their gifts of the spirit and ultimately shut them down.

Those that are anointed with the spirit of Elijah will always have to overcome the spirit of Jezebel sometime in their lives. Life can become especially grievous for them if that person happens to be their spouse whom they love greatly yet now is their primary enemy. On one hand they want to honor their spouse and live in unity of spirit with them, but can Elijah live in unity and tolerate Jezebel? Unfortunately the answer to that question is no. There is a constant battle going on in the marriage that is a continual state of strife that can feel unbearable to endure for yet one more day. The situation grows continually worse for the victim after enduring years of control, manipulation and deceit. The spouse feels hopeless after years of battling the person who is supposed to be their loving spouse. It can feel as if they are dealing directly with Jezebel as the words that are spoken to them by the enemy cut them to the core. In most cases those that are suffering with Jezebel is extremely anointed once completely set free and will experience a great breakthrough in their circumstances and in ministry. Jezebel is evil and wicked to the core causing the afflicted person to behave opposite of a true Christian and will do everything it can to maintain control so that neither spouse will reach the potential that God has for them.

The Jezebel afflicted person has probably experienced a tremendous amount of strife with their spouse(s) and children yet will claim very little if any responsibility for it by placing most of the blame on their controlled spouse saying "you never admit to sharing in the responsibility for the strife in our marriage." In reality the responsibility of all strife within the relationship falls squarely upon the Jezebel controlled person. Yet most counselors would side with the Jezebel controlled person's explanation of the strife being their spouse because Jezebel knows how to sell it so well. The counselors will typically agree that "both spouses should take their fair share of the blame as everyone knows that all relationships are 50/50 in blame." as one ignorant pastor explained who actually had Jezebel himself. This is just not the case when it involves the Jezebel spirit. Jezebel seeks to marry a compliant, meek and loving person who is easy to control and dominate, thus they cause the lion's share of strife in the marriage. Control is often exerted by threats over many years if they ever tell anyone how they have been abusive and controlling over their spouse.

Keep in mind we are talking about the Jezebel spirit in a person who could be very loving and kind to everyone else in the world yet will destroy their own spouse or children due to hearing the voices of the enemy. Also remember that most of the people that have the Jezebel spirit at a strong level are usually going to be extremely anointed by the Lord as soon as they recognize that they have that spirit affecting them and no longer want it and effectively command it to go. Many will be blessed with amazingly impactful ministries that will save thousands upon thousands of lives for Christ once Jezebel's victim is set free.

It is very helpful to see just what damage a Jezebel controlled person is capable of doing to their loved ones. The purpose of these examples is to show just what the spirit can do to good people at heart and yet when the spirit gains control of them how it can do some extremely evil things. An innocent looking person you would never suspect was capable of such destruction, when under the control of Jezebel can do the unimaginable.

An anointed husband with strong faith, seeing many physical healings in his life and others he prayed for, once developed a small bulge on his spine that his daughter, wife and step-son noticed when they went swimming. He was not worried as he knew his authority in Christ when it came to being healed by the Lord. He had been healed from everything for the past five years as he became more aware of his identity in Christ and the authority given to him by Jesus to heal the sick. Two months later the bulge began to grow rapidly over just a few days to the size of a golf ball. He was still not worried or in fear because he knew God would heal him of it. He didn't show the larger bulge to his wife because he knew she did not have much faith in healings and was more likely to become fearful and worried. He commanded the bulge to dissolve but after one month it had not gone. There was no fear or worry on his part as he knew it had to go away eventually because "by His stripes we are healed." It was simply an annoyance that he knew God would heal at some point so he waited for the healing to manifest in the physical and dissolve the bulge. He slept on it night after night and it was very painful. When he drove a car he could feel pain on his back against the seatback but his wife never knew as he kept it hidden from her. His wife's oldest son hugged him once and could feel the larger bulge protruding from his back because it was protruding noticeably. At the same time his wife started having blurring in her vision and was thinking she may need to go to the doctor.

So he asked the Lord what was going on and God told him that his wife needed to be in more unity with him in spirit to see that He would heal him of the painful bulge because of something in her life that would be similar and occur in the near future and that if she would pray for him he would be healed. Also at the same time if he prayed for his wife she would be healed of her vision problems. So he finally showed his wife his back and she was shocked and said he should have gone to the doctor (instead of commanding the healing so Jesus could heal). He told her God would heal him when she prayed and that she would no longer have blurry vision after he prayed for her. So they both prayed for each other. She stopped having blurry vision immediately. However his bulge in his back stayed the size of a golf ball for several more days but he did not get in fear as he knew what God had promised him. Several days later the bulge finally started getting smaller little by little and after three weeks it was completely gone. It was most likely a cyst but since he never went to the doctor it could have been a tumor or other painful growth the size of a golf ball.

Two months later his wife came against him as they were driving in the car and challenged him on his faith and asked him what he thought his faith for healings was compared to her as she did

58

not want him to have stronger faith than she and was very jealous. He felt very uncomfortable in answering the question because he knew if he told the truth that she would get very angry with him but if he lied and said she had the same faith then that would not be truthful. So he told her that his faith was a little stronger than hers and she still got mad and said "see you think you are better than me" and went on and on about him being too proud and verbally berated him for being too high and mighty for over an hour. He was grieved that she would try to compete with him on faith and wanted her to be on the same level or even more than he, but he knew the enemy in her was strong and always competing and never at peace or supportive. He wanted her to be on the same page but knew this was not possible as her continual strife, verbal and physical abuse was still a large issue so he just continued to suffer in silence.

Two months later his wife felt a pain in her lower region and attended a Christian conference with him and a couple of other friends. Then an anointed man that was one of the main speakers prayed for healing over the 3,000 people that attended and she felt her pain get healed. Many people came forward and several announced they were healed to the crowd including his wife who testified to everyone there. Yet the next day after the conference she was back to verbally harassing and berating her husband with her words for hours and hours in the car and then the next morning her pain returned and worsened. She called her husband while he was working out at the gym and said she thought she may need to go to the doctor. He said he would take her to the doctor but asked if he could pray for her first and give God a chance to heal her. He had been seeing many healed through his prayers and they had both been healed of every physical ailment for the previous 5 ½ years after they learned about their authority in Christ for healing and how to pray effectively commanding the infirmity to go in Jesus name instead of pleading with God to do it. Unfortunately she became angry that he asked to pray for her and said no and that she would call her family to come get her and take her to the doctor and hung up on him in anger. This grieved him because he knew she would try to make him look like he was heartless and mean instead of the truth that she would not give God a chance to heal her before he took her to the doctor. So by the time he arrived home she refused to allow him to take her to the doctor in order for him to look bad as her family member was arriving shortly to take her.

She then later told her family and other mutual friends that he refused to take her to the doctor which of course was not true because she wanted to make him look bad in their eyes. He did not learn that she had told them until many months later when a mutual friend of theirs had asked if it was true that he had actually refused to take her to the doctor. After the doctor visit, she was contacted to go to a hospital to remove what turned out to be a cyst which was most likely the same thing he had on his back just a few months before. Upon leaving the hospital after surgery she told her husband privately as they walked out of the hospital together "you must promise me you will stop doing ministry and focus on me and our marriage." He reluctantly agreed, even though he did nothing wrong and wanted to continue to pray for people to be healed and do what the Lord wanted him to do.

The Jezebel spirit in her wanted to come against him in ministry in order to shut him down, which is exactly what Jezebel does, especially to those that operate in the prophetic or healing gifts. That week she treated him harshly, much like a slave, while he waited on her hand and foot. He made dinner, helped her with baths, and poured out his love on her to help her recover while she berated him verbally. Later, she wanted prayer at their church for healing after she had the surgery. When he took her to the church the leader of the healing rooms asked him to help out in one of their rooms because they needed a man to accompany the women in the prayer room. He had worked in the healing rooms up until his wife demanded that he stop doing ministry the week prior.

He wasn't planning to minister because he knew his wife would be angry with him for going against her demand yet he wanted to do the Lord's work. He reluctantly agreed since he knew it would not take time away from their marriage because his wife was receiving prayer in another room. A man came into his room for prayer with a ruptured disk in his back that needed surgery having had extreme pain for almost a year and after he prayed for the man God instantly healed him. The healed man then told everyone at the church about his healing which his wife overheard. On the drive home she was furious that he had "ministered" to the man and screamed saying "You promised to not minister anymore!" He pleaded that he did not take any time away from their marriage because she was there for prayer yet she reminded him he promised not to do any ministry until she allowed him. Over and over she ranted and raged, furious that he actually defied her demand.

A week later she told him he could no longer sleep in his bed with her to exert greater control over him so he told her that he would most likely need to move out from her like her previous three husbands had done before him. She mocked him saying he would never move out since he had endured her control for many years and kept the abuse a secret as she had threatened him repeatedly. He prayed about it and God told him to separate as He would finish what he started by setting his wife free from the controlling spirits by bringing herself to the end and causing her circumstances to get worse. God would also bless him greatly in ministry in order that all the people she told lies to would ultimately know the truth by the fruit. Everything in his heart did not want to move out because he loved her and wanted her healed but he knew if he stayed he would be completely cut off from all ministry by her and stopped from any interactions with others in ministry or at church. He also knew he would become completely emasculated as a man of God and be subject to depression and hopelessness as the demonic spirit in her hated the Holy Spirit in him.

He moved out of their home and within a few weeks he learned for the first time, why his wife had been so horrible to him for the six years they were married. A mutual friend of theirs discerned that she had the Jezebel spirit afflicting her. He began to research the Jezebel spirit and discovered that indeed she had manifested almost all possible behavior traits of that spirit. Shortly after that time, the Lord started to bless him greatly as he began seeing hundreds of miraculous physical healings of people he prayed for. Many people who had the Jezebel spirit started coming to him every month and he was able to lead them through renunciation prayers to command the spirits to go. Lives were forever changed and their marriages restored, many instantly. The truth eventually became evident over time to the very same people who had heard the lies of his wife and had initially believed them. Jezebel is extremely controlling and evil and can make good people do very controlling and wicked things to their spouses and children. It is important to look at the actual fruit of the person speaking them over time and discern the spirits that are on them. Be careful to not take what they say at face value because those with the Jezebel spirit will lie to your face and if you are not discerning, you will not know the truth! It is truly a life of unwanted torment for the person with the Jezebel spirit and more so for their victim spouse/children or friends and for all the people that stand in their way.

Another man's wife that had Jezebel broke every window in her home and then called the police and told them that her husband broke all the windows and had him arrested. He landed in jail because they believed the woman over her husband because they are adept at lying and act the victim role very convincingly. Justice was not served for a good man who was desperately trying to survive the onslaught of lies proliferated by the spirit of Jezebel.

One man's wife was staying with him at the Huntington Beach, CA Hyatt Regency Resort & Spa and he was trying to sleep but she continued to "rant and rage" and verbally berate him with words from the enemy. After an hour of enduring this tirade (which she had done for many years to him) he decided to get out of bed and walk away out of the room. As he walked out of the room she followed him demanding that he come back. He ignored her demand and then she tried to grab him to make him come back so he had to run away from her. She chased him through the hallways and finally he had to run to a stairwell and change floors but she continued to chase him. After ten minutes of being chased he finally lost her and just sat in a stairwell at the other end of the resort hiding under the lowest floor's stair and just cried to the Lord for hours pleading with Him to heal his wife and get her to change and treat him humanely. But the Lord would not heal her yet as He was preparing him to lead others to their healings from this horrendous spirit years later. Sometimes the Lord allows us go through extreme pain for a season of years in order to help thousands upon thousands of souls later. It is not fun going through the season of pain but it is definitely worth it when you are able to help the lives of many that are being tortured by their spouses by helping them to freedom, deliverance, and restoration of their lives and marriages.

In yet another example of the Jezebel spirit, a woman had berated her husband for over three hours straight exhausting him from listening to her evil words and when she finally stopped he got ready for bed. Shockingly to him she wanted to be intimate (because that spirit is very selfish and all about satisfying their own carnal desires) and he told her politely that he was not capable of doing that (for the first time in their marriage after five years that he had told her no) as he was exhausted from all of the onslaught of words that he had just taken and needed to rest. So he laid down in bed and closed his eyes to sleep. Within seconds his wife was furious that she could not have her selfish carnal desires met so she picked up a large drinking glass and threw it at him missing his head by about three feet as it smashed into the wall next to his bed shattering into pieces and making a large dent in the drywall. He was shocked and looked at his wife and asked what was wrong with her and he could see extreme hatred in her eyes for him. A strong Jezebel spirit in a person can be extremely demanding when it comes to her sexual desires and will strike out if she does not get what she wants, when she wants it. So if you are married to a full-fledged Jezebel you will face the wrath of his/her perverted desires many times and will become worn out from giving him/her what they want whenever they want it or they will restrict you and it will be mechanical and void of all love. It is not a loving and pure sexual desire whatsoever and there is nothing good in it for their victim.

Another man had endured more verbal abuse from his wife than he could take and he wanted her to stop but she would not. So finally out of exasperation he decided to walk out of the house to get away from the situation. His wife ran outside and was waiting for him by his car that was parked on their driveway in broad daylight and lunged at him grabbing both his arms with her hands. He was much stronger than she was but the demonic strength inside of her was more than he could overcome. He struggled to get free for many minutes before finally being able to get her to lose the grip by bending down and getting his shirt to come off over his head. He then ran back into the house to get a new shirt and she chased him. Then he ran out the back patio door and she ran after him. He tried to get into his car before she could grab him but could not as she grabbed both of his arms again and held on tightly. He tried to close the door carefully so as not to hurt her but she would not let go. He closed it a little harder each time but still she would not release him. He had to close it several more times before she finally relented and gave up. So then he started his car and began to back up only to see that she was now standing behind his vehicle to stop him from leaving. She had done this several times before when his car was in their garage trying to get away from her to stop him from leaving and each time he would give up and not leave. Determined to leave, this time he knew if he went slow enough she would have to get out of the way and eventually she did. He drove away and cried out for hours to the Lord to help get his wife free from whatever was causing her to behave this way for all these years but the Lord did not intervene in the deliverance. Then over a year later the woman's husband separated from her. She could not stand to lose control so in her desire to gain it back she filed a protective order against him but could not come up with "charges" in order to sell it to a judge. She lied and blamed him on the order saying that he was the one that grabbed her arms and would not let go saying that he would later blame her for it. Her husband just let it go and did not fight it because He trusted the Lord would reveal the truth later and that he would eventually be exonerated since he did nothing wrong to her.

One woman's husband that had the Jezebel spirit learned that her husband had spoken lies to the leaders at her church in order to gain their support. She never knew what was happening until she had to separate from him and eventually was given revelation about the damage that he had already done months in advance and learned that he lied about many things. Later when he was told that he had the Jezebel spirit he initially denied it and blamed his spouse as having that spirit but a few weeks later he had the revelation that he indeed did have it and disclosed about how the enemy spoke to him and how selfish he was and how much fear he had in him that was driving his controlling behavior and his lies.

Another woman said her mother had the Jezebel spirit and would always cause strife by verbally starting fights, provoking contention and then blaming her daughter. It was very frustrating for the daughter to be around her mother her entire life and she had to escape for peace.

Another man had loved on his wife's two grown sons by allowing them to live in their home after she moved in with her husband. He allowed them to pay a below market rent amount and no utilities for five years with one year not charging any rent because her son lost his job. He also paid various other bills that her sons could not afford on their own including a 3D TV, school loans, credit card bills, car repair expenses, phone bills, living expenses, giving his own personal vehicle to one son for 9 months so he could do his job, etc. He paid over $85,000 in five years for them to show them true unconditional love and expected nothing to be repaid. When she continued to control him and tried to stop him from doing ministry he separated from her and then she charged all her living expenses on a mutual credit card that he was paying each month. He continued to pay the credit card and for all her utilities. She kept all of the money that she was making from her business. She would never offer to help pay for anything and had finally hit the credit limit on the card. Eventually when he could no longer keep up with paying for all her bills and needed her to help with an electric bill from her home and a mutual credit card payment totaling $1,000 he texted her asking if it would be acceptable to take the money out of a joint account where she deposited $1,000 from her work to pay for her bills. She did not reply. So since he wanted to take care of her he took the money out of their joint bank account in order to pay her bills on time. She later became angry and furious that he took "her" money out and told her father. The father called him and left a threatening message on his cell phone that he would "find him" to return the money. The husband had no money to return because he had paid her bills with it. Within that week she filed for divorce from him and told others he stole her money and other lies to sell the divorce to her church leadership. Jezebel causes a person to be extremely selfish and controlling and never takes any responsibility herself, always blaming their spouse.

One man loved his wife since she was in school but had to wait to marry her until after she had been with several other men. She actually had three different children from three different men. Once he married her she started to abuse him verbally and it soon became physical – running towards him at full speed one time outside trying to tackle him. He kept trying to get her to stop and told her she loved him but she never would change and she would be mean to her children. Then one day after many horrible incidents he came home and noticed she had a booklet on abuse and rape on the kitchen table. Then a day later she had a police investigator interrogate him about allegations against him which were not true and the police decided to put him in jail. Fortunately and miraculously later his wife was convicted for lying about him and told the police that she lied. They would not allow him to get out of jail and kept him locked up for a year. Also the man had a cell mate whose girlfriend he caught having sex with another man in his own bed and his girlfriend accused him of raping her. The police locked him up and later his girlfriend admitted that she lied but they would not allow him out of jail after she told the truth.

One man who had a very strong and devious Jezebel spirit engaged several anointed men who were involved in very effective ministries that were growing and being blessed by the Lord. He acted like he was a multi-millionaire and said he helped to fund ministries around the world and came up with many testimonies and stories that sounded very convincing. He promised the men that he would pay them large salaries and was arranging it with his other multi-millionaire friends and they would be paid in just a few months. He required that they spend time with him as much as possible which involved attending breakfasts starting at 8:00 am that would involve the man boasting about the same god miracle stories over and over and ultimately conclude around 2:00 or 3:00 pm. He would want them to come to as many of these breakfasts / Bible studies as possible and some would try to come to them 3 days a week. All of the men's time to operate in their own ministries or jobs to produce income was being taken from them more and more as he continued to hold a carrot of having all their bills paid and making more money than they could imagine and do ministry with him and his growing ministry around the world. Ultimately the man tried telling them that he was going to build a huge multi-million dollar facility that would encompass all of their ministries to work with people from around the world but when finally they asked when they would start getting paid by him he twisted scripture to say that they should freely give their services and not expect any salaries. So the Jezebel in him was very sly for months as he appeared that he was a very giving man when in reality he lied about everything he said and tried to derail their ministries. God taught them all a valuable lesson and that was not to be pulled into what appeared to be an amazing ministry with the promise of a lot of money but to listen to the Holy Spirit and continue on course.

One woman was so desperate for the love of her controlling and rejecting father that she married her second husband against her will. Her father spoke to the pastor that was counseling them to have the pastor counsel his daughter to agree to the marriage because he was concerned she might go back to her first husband that she loved. The father viewed the first husband as a bad man. So she married the second husband and recounted it was a nightmare that fortunately ended two years later when he also divorced her. Her mother finally admitted years later that her father was wrong for forcing her to marry him but her father never admitted that he was wrong. Then later her father coerced her to divorce her fourth husband who had separated from her in order to get her to treat him with love and proper respect instead of control and abuse. So she divorced the only husband that loved her like Christ as he took much abuse from her, and the only one that she truly loved, in order to get some acceptance from her controlling father. That is how desperate a Jezebel controlled woman can be for the love of her father as she will spend a lifetime trying to be accepted by her father. She also seeks to punish the spouse as a surrogate for the father she is angry with. So the sins of her father become transferred onto her husband and the pain and anger she has stored up from her youth gets discharged upon her Godly husband, the sacrificial lamb. Ephesians 5:25 NKJV says *"[25] Husbands, love your wives, just as Christ loved the church and gave himself up for her [26] to make her holy, cleansing her by the washing with water through the word, [27] and to present her to himself as a radiant church, without stain or wrinkle or any other blemish, but holy and blameless."* There is nothing more extreme then to try to love a person affected by the Jezebel spirit.

The Jezebel afflicted person is extreme in her controlling ways but also usually knows a lot of scripture in the Bible to manipulate in order to get their way. Yet they do not behave lovingly to their spouse or children in private and are extremely controlling which contradicts scripture of how we are to love our spouse and family. If the abused spouse truly has the Spirit of Elijah anointing, they will break free through an eventual separation and rise up against the spirit of Jezebel any way they can in order to help their spouse gain freedom. Sadly, many will simply divorce because they have given up all hope of seeing a change and any attempts at counseling are futile. Jezebel will not be honest in counseling and the cycle will continue for the Jezebel afflicted person as they look for a new victim to control and dominate again and again. They do not know how to love as their father and or mother never showed them love.

Can the victim spouse deliver their own controlling spouse from the Jezebel spirit? No – because Jezebel will not listen to them and will have such anger and contempt for them that nothing will come through the filter that they view them through. Therefore the victim spouse will need a Jehu to come alongside and help them confront their Jezebel spouse with the truth. This book and the Holy Spirit will help be your Jehu to truly allow the afflicted Jezebel spouse to have their eyes opened to the truth of what really happened to them in childhood and admit that they do have the spirit that is speaking to them and causing them to behave in a controlling manner. That is 90% of the battle – to admit that they have the spirit then lastly, have the person command the spirit to go themselves. Later in this book I have included powerfully effective prayers which have been used successfully thousands of times to command the spirits to go with amazing and instant results.

So just who was Jezebel in the Old Testament? It is important to know the history of the woman that took on the moniker for these insidious behaviors.

Scripture References—1 Kings 16:31; 18:4-19; 19:1, 2; 21:5-25; 2 Kings 9

The spirits of control, deceit, seduction, witchcraft and murder which came against God's anointed were operating in the world long before the woman who exemplified these spirits was born. Queen Jezebel symbolized the combined capabilities of all these spirits better than anyone and thus naming this spirit after her was most appropriate. Bible Gateway does a great job of explaining more in detail about the woman of Jezebel. This scheming and evil woman with a history of murder truly represented the spirit that bore her name as by nature she was a most proud, immoral, manipulative and even murderous woman. She was a seductress, using all the ploys of a sensual woman trying to lure in her prey using all her methods both physically and emotionally. Jezebel was rejected by her father and had a controlling mother.

She was the daughter of Ethbaal, king of the Zidonians, and priest of Baal worshipers. The Phoenicians were an extraordinary race, and outstanding as the great sea faring peoples of the ancient world, but they were idolaters who regarded God as only a local deity, "the god of the land." Their gods were Baal and Ashtaroth or Astarte, with their innumerable number of priests, 450 of whom Ahab used in the amazing temple to the Sun-god he had built in Samaria. Another 400 priests were housed in a sanctuary that Jezebel built for them, and whom she provided food from her own table. Perverse and evil rites were associated with the worship of Baal including child sacrifice.

It was this ungodly woman who married Ahab who was the king of Northern Israel, and who in so doing was guilty of a rash and damaging act which resulted in evil consequences. As a Jew, Ahab sinned against his own Hebrew faith by taking as his wife the daughter of a man whose very name, Ethbaal, meant, "A Man of Baal." Ahab was captivated by her beauty and commanding character and fell for her, and Jezebel, cunning and proud, eagerly seized the opportunity of sharing the throne of a king.

Any man, able to resist the wiles of a beautiful but wicked woman possesses true heroism. Joseph succeeded against the lovely yet lustful wife of Potiphar, but Caesar and Antony after conquering almost the whole world, were conquered by Cleopatra. The Welsh revival in 1904 saw over 100,000 souls come to the Lord through a young man named Evan Roberts but he was conquered by a Jezebel controlled woman named Jesse Penn-Lewis who seduced and deceived the revivalist in the prime of his anointing in the early 1920's. She sought to ride on Roberts' coattails and flattered him with her words that tried to ease the pain he was suffering from the religious spirits coming against the revival. But her smooth words hurt and did not help him. He suffered a nervous breakdown and was confined to a bed for more than a year and he allowed his wife to decide who he would see and what he would do. She wrote a book called "War on the Saints" that he later denounced. Her doctrine was largely rejected in Wales. Although Roberts lived to 72 he ceased preaching in his early 20's. Jezebel hates the move of the Holy Spirit and shut the revival down just as it was really starting to move powerfully.

Ahab, enchanted by Jezebel, took her to be his wife, and served Baal and worshipped him. All the other sins of Ahab were minor as compared to his marriage to Jezebel and serving Baal that followed. 1 Kings 16:30-32 NKJV states *"[30] Now Ahab the son of Omri did evil in the sight of the Lord, more than all who were before him. ³¹ And it came to pass, as though it had been an insignificant thing for him to walk in the sins of Jeroboam the son of Nebat that he took as wife Jezebel the daughter of Ethbaal, king of the Sidonians and he went and served Baal and worshiped him. ³² Then he set up an altar for Baal in the temple of Baal, which he had built in Samaria."* For over 60 years idolatry had made a horrible life for the Hebrews and meant more to them than the breaking of the first two commandments of the law; it produced spiritual and moral disintegration which was intensified by Jezebel's determined effort to destroy the worship of the one and true God. What was the character of Jezebel? Her name has become a prominent cliché for seductive power, worldly subtlety and evil of the worst type throughout the ages.

Jezebel was no ordinary woman who was misguided through an error in judgment. Her behavior caused her to attract the immediate attention of all that came into her presence. Though by no means a sweet and loving person, she had a masculine and militaristic demand of others, and was dominated by her extraordinary force of character. Jezebel's life came to an awful fate with a just ending which belongs to no other woman of the Bible. While the Bible does not go into great detail about her character, it simply sets forth the events in which she bore such a major part, yet as we read between the lines we see her as a woman of powerful force, intellect, and will. She knew nothing of the restraint of higher pure principles. Savage and relentless, this proud and strong-minded woman carried out her foul schemes and whoever got in her way would face a terrible ending. A skillful woman, she prostituted all her gifts for the continuance of evil, and her misused talents became a curse. Persuasive, her influence was wrongly directed. Nothing would or could stop her in the flesh. Unyielding above other women, she used her strength of character to destroy a king and her own descendants, as well as corrupt the life of an entire nation.

Baal had no more devoted follower than Jezebel. None could match her desire for the worship of Ashtaroth the famous goddess of the Zidonians, as zealous and liberal maintenance of hundreds of idolatrous priests clearly proves. Not content with establishing the idol worship of her own country in her husband's court, she desired to convert the entire nation of Israel to Baal worship. Two heathen sanctuaries were built, one at Samaria with its 450 priests, and the other at Jezreel with its 400 priests. In a most relentless fashion Jezebel tried to drive out the true prophets of God from the land, and thus became the first religious female persecutor in history by using the power that was given to her by her husband King Ahab. From her idolatrous father, a high priest of Ashtaroth, she inherited her fanatical religious enthusiasm which inspired her to exterminate the worship of the true and living God, and almost succeeded in the attempt.

The overtaking of the nation with all the sins and cruel superstitions of such a discouraging cult as Baalism brought upon the scene the chief of the true prophets, Elijah. He appeared suddenly before Ahab, predicted three years of drought, and at the end of the period unexpectedly appeared again and challenged the 850 prophets of Baal to a supreme test of power. The confrontation took place at the top of Mount Carmel which today overlooks the valley of Megiddo which is to be the place of the final battle of Armageddon that will take place during the end times before the second coming of Christ. Elijah taunted them making fun of their gods for sleeping and then with great boldness commanded fire to fall from heaven and then took back the control from Jezebel and had the people kill all the priests of Baal while Ahab escaped back home to Jezebel to report on what happened.

After such an overwhelming victory, once Elijah heard about Jezebel's threat (which is a very common ploy to be threatened by people who host the Jezebel spirit which cause fear in their victims) to kill Elijah and his partners "by tomorrow at this time" caused him to fear and he felt that the fury of a murderous woman was more than he could face. The spirit of controlling fear caused him to flee for his life across the kingdom of Judah, leaving the arrogant queen, for the time being, in undeniable possession of the land.

Ahab was like a puppet in the hands of his overpowering wife. He was compliant and weak which made it easy for Jezebel to achieve her murderous designs. How could worthless and spineless Ahab resist the evil scheming of his immoral partner? It was Jezebel who became feared commander in Israel and not the cowardly husband she could put under her thumb. Ahab was more luxury-loving and sensual than cruel, but under the complete domination of a ruthless woman he was forced to act against his finer feelings. Without Ahab's authority, Jezebel would have been a serpent without fangs. In this marriage, Ahab was the weaker vessel with a wife who mocked his diligent scruples and bound him in all wickedness as with strong chains.

Our Lord used a striking figure to illustrate the continuing influence of evil, emanating from a life devoid of godly principles—

Do men gather grapes of thorns, or figs of thistles? ... a corrupt tree brings forth evil fruit.... a corrupt tree cannot bring forth good fruit (Matthew 7:16-20).

Jezebel had a rotten root and so everything connected with her was contaminated. With her strength of character, lust for power, remorseless rejection of godliness, and unshrinking and resolute activity to eliminate all that interferes with the satisfaction of her wicked designs, she was evil in every imaginable way.

Her children continued in the wickedness in which they were raised. Jezebel's evil influence was revived in her daughter Athaliah of Judea. Her maligned character reappears in her eldest son, Ahaziah, who, like his idolatrous mother, was a devout worshiper of Baal. Her second son, Jehoram or Joram, was another image of his mother—further corrupt fruit from a corrupt tree. It was Jehoram, who heard from the lips of Jehu who had been raised up to obliterate the Ahab dynasty, that there would be no peace in Israel, "so long as the whoredoms of thy mother Jezebel and her witchcrafts are so many" (2 Kings 9:22). Is it to be pondered that Jehoram suffered a similar fate to that of his mother's at the hands of Jehu?

The tragedy of Naboth and his vineyard reveals how vicious a woman Jezebel was. Life was cheap to such a female who had murder in her veins. Her father, Ethbaal, murdered his predecessor, Phelles. Brought up in such a home of intrigue and murder, what else could we expect but a she-devil as Jezebel had become?

Naboth's refusal was the introduction to one of the strangest, most powerful, and most terrible stories of the Bible; a drama, on the one side, of innocence, courage, independence, and the fear of God, and, on the other side, of covetousness, greediness, cruelty, perjury, death and terrible revenge.

Jezebel was prepared to murder in her stride toward the desired objective, as the incident of Naboth's vineyard reveals. King Ahab happened to see this fruitful vineyard and inquired as to its owner. Learning it belonged to Naboth; Ahab called him to the palace and offered to buy the vineyard. But it was not for sale. It had belonged to his forefathers and had become precious to Naboth, and as an Israelite Ahab understood his desire to retain it. Thwarted in what he coveted, Ahab took to his bed and fasted.

Jezebel came upon the scene. Learning what had happened, and, as a foreigner from a country where the wishes of a king were never questioned, she revealed herself as a woman of accumulated authority when she consoled Ahab by saying—

"Arise and eat bread, and let thine heart be merry. I will give thee the vineyard of Naboth the Jezreelite."

Jezebel ordered, by letter, stamped with the royal seal, a public feast. She also instituted an assembly of the people of Jezreel to try the pure and Godly Naboth for blasphemies against God and the king. Naboth was arrested, tried and convicted on the accounts of false witnesses secured by Jezebel. She found these witnesses in order to appear within the bounds of the law. Found guilty, Naboth was stoned until his innocent life was crushed out of him. Ahab took possession of the much-coveted vineyard. But the blood of godly Naboth did not cry out in vain. God called Elijah out of his retirement to go to Ahab and pronounce the fearful doom awaiting the murderous pair and their unholy seed. The prophet told the king of his fate—

"In the place where the dogs licked the blood of Naboth, shall dogs lick thy blood, even thine."

This prophecy was fulfilled shortly after its pronouncement for war broke out between the Israelites and the Syrians, and Ahab, while riding in his chariot, received his death wound. The blood-soaked chariot was taken to the spring which ran through Naboth's vineyard, and the dogs came and licked up the bloody water. Concerning Jezebel, Elijah said, "The dogs shall eat Jezebel by the wall of Jezreel," and shortly we shall see how this prophecy was also fulfilled to the very letter.

The death of Ahab, the one whom Jezebel had "stirred up to work wickedness in the sight of the Lord" revealed her to be proud and unable to have any feelings of repentance. There was no sign of sorrow in her, as she went out proudly to meet her prophesied doom. Jehu had been appointed and anointed as the avenger of God, and he set about his grim task of dealing out justice to those who had polluted the land. Jezebel's son and grandson met Jehu in the blood-stained vineyard Naboth had once possessed. Jehu killed Jezebel's son, the king of Israel, and her grandson was overtaken while trying to get away and was killed. The still proud, defiant queen-mother knew her last hour was not far away, and great-grandmother though she was, she took time to arrange her hair and paint her face, and looked out at a window to greet Jehu as he passed by. Jezebel did not paint her face from any motive of vanity because she knew that death was ready to finally take her. Therefore, she determined to die like a queen....so Jezebel painted her eyes and placed her jeweled crown upon her head; then, mounting to the palace tower, she watched the impressive advance of Jehu's chariot.

One item in her sinful life that gave rise to the bitter taunt, "a painted Jezebel," as painting the face was accepted as evidence that a woman had loose morals. Certainly no woman's name in history has become as commonly accepted as a symbol for wickedness.

The climax came as Jehu entered the city gate. Reaching the palace, he looked up to the window from which came the taunting voice of Jezebel: "Is it peace, thou Zimri, thou murderer of thy master?" Such a taunt angered her triumphant enemy, and seeing the two eunuchs standing at the window with the defiant queen he shouted up to them, "Who is on my side? Who? Throw her down!"

They obeyed and threw her out of the window, and as she fell the walls were sprinkled with her blood. Below her were the soldiers with their spears, the horses to tread her underfoot and the hungry dogs waiting for her flesh. The triumphant Jehu entered the palace over Jezebel's dead body. As he ate and drank where she was just standing, he remembered that the one who had just died as prophesied had been a queen and a mother of kings, so he ordered—

"Go, see now this cursed woman, and bury her. And they went to bury her, but they found no more of her than the skull, and the feet, and the palms of her hands."

So Jezebel perished, the idolater, the tyrant, the murderess. She had sown to the wind, and reaped the whirlwind. Many of the godly in Israel must have felt that while Jezebel held evil influence over the land, the deliverance by God seemed to come slowly. But God's retribution eventually did come. Thus Jezebel encountered a "mysterious, terrible and divine reckoning."

As we turn from our picture of one of the most wicked women who ever breathed, there are one or two lessons to learn from her deeply tainted record. No matter from what angle we approach the life of Jezebel, she stands out as an example to both nations and individuals that the wages of sin is truly death. Further, from this great tragic figure of the Bible we learn how important it is for the influence of a wife and mother to be on the side of all that is good and noble. As Ahab's evil genius, Jezebel was the absolute denial of all God meant a woman to be, namely, a true help-mate of man who was loving and nurturing and supportive. Ahab, as we read, was "stirred up" by Jezebel but stirred up in the wrong direction. When a man marries a woman because of her beauty or forceful personality, or marries a wicked woman or one opposed to his religion, he usually brings sorrow, heartache and disappointment. Jezebel retained her obstinate, inflexible character to the very end. The death of the man whose life she contaminated brought no repentance. What a different story could have been written if only she had learned how to stir up her husband and children to love God and follow good works (2 Timothy 1:6; 2 Peter 1:13). Her misdirected talents, however, brought upon her a curse. The evil she perpetrated was done under the guise of religion.

Finally, evil, witchcraft, and godlessness bring their own reward, and the wicked reap what they sow. Justice overtook Jezebel when her body was thrown out of the window to be torn and mangled, and then eaten by dogs. As a daughter of the devil, she suffers a worse retribution in the realms of the doomed.

There are those who reject such a lurid description of the fate of the wicked who, like Jezebel, defy and deny God, but the divine Word still stands, that Christ is to be revealed from heaven to take vengeance on those who spurn God and who reject the saving Gospel of His beloved Son.

2 Thessalonians 1:5-10 NKJV *"5 which is manifest evidence of the righteous judgment of God, that you may be counted worthy of the kingdom of God, for which you also suffer; 6 since it is a righteous*

thing with God to repay with tribulation those who trouble you,[7] and to give you who are troubled rest with us when the Lord Jesus is revealed from heaven with His mighty angels, [8] in flaming fire taking vengeance on those who do not obey the gospel of our Lord Jesus Christ. [9] These shall be punished with everlasting destruction from the presence of the Lord and from the Glory of His power, [10] when He comes, in that Day, to be glorified in His saints and to be admired among all those who believe, because our testimony among you was believed."

Several have asked the question....can a person truly host all that is a part of the Jezebel spirit and be a pure and loving Christian at the same time? Although they are able to hear from the Lord at times and even give prophetic words that are right on – they also hear from the enemy spirit often which causes them to behave contrary to the Holy Spirit. Thus they behave like a Jekyll and Hyde to their spouse and children and potentially other victims. It is truly a tormented state for them and their loved ones to live in. If you have a strong gift of discernment in the spirit you can see when the spirit of Jezebel is on an individual as their face looks fake and deceptive and they will overact like they are loving and sweet while being put off by people that they believe are beneath them. There will be times though when the person feels convicted by being around a person who is strong in the Lord and can see through them into their spirit that the person will break down in tears and know that the person knows the truth about them. That is the real person that is then coming through of who they are without the spirit affecting them. Often times you may only see the real side of who they are in Christ just 25% of the time. Sometimes if they are not as affected by Jezebel you may see it 50-75% of the time. The point is to be discerning and wise and truly help them to be able to see the Jezebel spirit influence in their lives and bring it to their attention in a loving and gentle way so they can get total freedom from their life of deception, lies and torment.

Chapter 6

So How Do You Gain Freedom?

So how do you get the Spirit of Jezebel to stop afflicting, controlling, and causing you to control and hurt others? I have found there are two types of versions of this spirit; the subtle / sly version and the more obvious aggressive / crazy version. Those that have had minimal pain inflicted on them from their father will have the subtle version while those that have received extreme control, rejection and pain from their father and mother will have the most extreme aggressive and scary version. Both have the underlying control, manipulation and deception and whispering lies behind your back about you to others but where the subtle version is less obvious to spot in a relationship the more aggressive version is dominant and can be physically and sexually abusive and will raise its voice many times over every day and be intimidating and dominating to cause fear in its victim. Both are not fun to be around but at least with the subtle version you can sleep at night without fear of a verbal barrage lasting for hours and things flying across the room smashing into the wall or windows or physical assaults. It is important to remember....if you are suffering from this spirit that you are not bad or evil....but the Spirit of Jezebel is extremely wicked and corrupt and is controlling your mind to cause you to serve its evil purposes and causing you to behave badly. Jezebel attacks those that are God's anointed prophets in order to keep them down for as long as possible. It is time for you to get free!

Generally, the younger you are, the easier it will be to admit that you may have this spirit and have a desire to command it to leave. The longer you "host" this spirit (say thirty or more years), the more it will want you to resist being delivered as it has become a stronghold in you mind for you which is much harder to break free from but not impossible with the help of the Holy Spirit and the insight in this book. You may deny that you have it, sometimes for months or years after you first are told you may have it. Often times you will try to get your church leadership to believe your lies so that you will be able to hold onto the Jezebel spirit longer. Leadership will then actually feel sorry for you instead of confronting you for your hosting that spirit and hurting your spouse, children and others. Churches that allow the gifts of the prophetic to flow and have people that attend who have those giftings often are afflicted strongly by multiple people with the Jezebel spirit and there will be much confusion, strife, and evil things that will begin happening if the people are allowed to keep the Jezebel spirit and operate in the church. It is a very awkward and confusing situation for those that are innocent and trying to keep peace in their church or ministry.

Most that have hosted Jezebel a long time will deny they have it as long as they can – but the Lord will bring circumstances into your life that will cause you to rethink holding on to the spirit (i.e. an increase in sickness and pain that never gets healed, multiple failed relationships and divorces, financial issues, things not going your way, more and more unusual difficult challenges, possibly even losing all you own if you still will not repent) to get you to see that the spirit is present in order for you to cry out to Him because you will finally want it gone. If you resist repentance, you eventually may feel like Jonah when he was in the belly of the whale. At some point because the Lord does not tolerate anyone that is trying to teach His people while operating in the Jezebel spirit, you will feel like you are taking on God Himself. It's like trying to live your life in a constant uphill battle in many ways, until you finally surrender. One man shared that for him it was like taking 2 steps forward, 3 steps back, 3 steps forward, 2 steps back for 8 months....and ultimately had to go on a 40 day water only fast in order to finally break it off of him. Another man initially told his counselor that he believed his wife had the Jezebel spirit to try to deflect it from himself and make his counselor believe she had it but eventually his circumstances became worse and he finally had to admit that he was the one that hosted it, as he was continuing to battle against the voices of the enemy that he had been hearing since a teenager but ultimately won out two months later.

Some women have suffered losing their spouses, families, ministries, jobs, homes, and suffering to the point of death before they realized how seriously important it was to renounce the spirit and truly be honest and repent once and for all and to take their authority over it and command it to be gone forever. Be aware that if you try to live a lie, your sins will eventually find you out. Unfortunately it may become very public in order to strip you of the pride and deceit into true humility and truth. You can either admit the truth and minimize the damage now privately or you can be exposed by the Lord publically and be completely and totally humbled – it is your choice.

Numbers 32:23 NJKV *"But if you do not do so, then take note, you have sinned against the Lord; and be sure your sin will find you out."*

Typical Christian counseling will not work with a person with Jezebel because the spirit will not be honest to the counselor and will twist the truth making themselves look innocent and thus your spouse will feel very frustrated dealing with your lies and twisting of the truth. Some people have gone to 40-50 counselors their whole lives and have never been set free because they lied to the counselors about themselves placing blame on their spouse(s) and conveying that they are blameless when in reality it was themselves that caused all their strife and contention in their marriage(s). They will insinuate that their spouse is not being honest in sharing the blame for marriage failure. Most counselors will agree with the Jezebel controlled person because it seems to make logical sense because Jezebel will twist the truth of the situation so that they look noble and will admit to just enough faults to make their victims look like they were lying because they would not agree to take half of the blame. Therefore if a trained counselor does not hear from the Lord they will be duped by Jezebel and the person will never be confronted or delivered and will continue living a life of lies, deception, control, manipulation, extreme strife and multiple divorces. Also 90% of all counselors and pastors do not even believe that the Jezebel spirit is real. The enemy loves that.

If the person has had the spirit a long time (i.e. 30 or more years) then it could take them many months or even years to completely surrender and be honest that they have it and want to get completely delivered as the spirit has had such a stronghold on their minds for a lifetime. Some may even hold on to the spirit and go forward with a divorce to their spouse that they really love who treated them as Godly as anyone could possibly have. Yet they do not want anyone to know the truth about how they lied and behaved as Jezebel does not want them to let go. One woman actually told her husband before they went to a pastor for counsel that he had to promise "not to say anything to the counselor that she did that was bad." The audacity of the Jezebel spirit is really amazing.

The truth usually comes out eventually over time as the fruit in a person's life becomes evident to all that really know both parties and observe what develops. If you are the victim spouse and are currently separated from your Jezebel spouse I would recommend trying to limit telling everyone in your church or community about the abuse from your spouse. Instead let the Holy Spirit slowly reveal the truth to others. What should you say if someone comes to you and asks why you separated? Ask the Holy Spirit what to do in your situation. Many have taken the stance to not contact anyone about what they endured but rather wait and if someone asks them - then they were released to share the truth in love. It is a delicate situation to a volatile problem because on one hand the Jezebel spirit will continue to thrive as long as people around them believe their lies but when the truth is revealed, then the Spirit of Jezebel loses its grip on them. So it is not an enjoyable experience to have to explain all the abuse to someone nor for the other party to hear the truth of the abuse of someone that they really love in Christ. It is difficult because the victim has been abused sometimes for many years and they will want the truth to finally come out so their spouse will be held accountable and change. Eventually many people will discern who is telling the truth over time by the fruit of each of their lives.

God knows what has happened no matter how many people your spouse has lied to about you and the truth will come out over time. No, it is not fun going to a church where half of them believe that the abused spouse was the "bad one" which is especially easy for people to believe if the abused was a man and his wife is telling the lies. Suffer as unto the Lord and He will have your back. Remember that lying is motivated by fear, which is contrary to love.

1 Peter 5:10 NKJV states *"But may the God of all grace, who called us to His eternal glory by Christ Jesus, after you have suffered a while, perfect, establish, strengthen, and settle you."* Luke 8:17 NJKV says *"For nothing is secret that will not be revealed, nor anything hidden that will not be known and come to light."*

Can you just love the person with the Jezebel spirit hoping they will change and be delivered? Unfortunately you cannot because Jezebel will take even more advantage of the person they are trying to control and flourish more in a church/ministry that does nothing to lovingly correct. To Jezebel love means "letting me do whatever I want and if you don't then you are controlling." Eventually you become so controlled by Jezebel that you begin to lose your identity as a person. If you are doing any ministry at all Jezebel will come against it and try to shut it down, causing their victims to feel totally under their thumb and broken of spirit. They will find some twisted way of making you not be effective in ministry. Therefore, the victim is forced to stand up for themselves and stand against Jezebel which is extremely hard to do as Jezebel's wrath will be poured out on her victim like none other.

Deliverance from the spirit can and must be done before the person should be allowed to do any ministry to others in or outside of the church. If the Jezebel person is currently in ministry it should be discontinued until the spirit is removed. The Lord is very serious about Jezebel and not allowing that spirit to be teaching or operating in the church until that spirit is removed and they are pure before the Lord:

Revelation 2:18-23 NKJV says *"18 And to the angel of the church in Thyatira write, 'These things says the Son of God, who has eyes like a flame of fire, and His feet like fine brass: 19 "I know your works, love, service, faith, and your patience; and as for your works, the last are more than the first. 20 Nevertheless I have a few things against you, because you allow that woman Jezebel, who calls herself a prophetess, to teach and seduce My servants to commit sexual immorality and eat things sacrificed to idols. 21 And I gave her time to repent of her sexual immorality, and she did not repent. 22 Indeed I will cast her into a sickbed, and those who commit adultery with her into great tribulation, unless they repent of their deeds. 23 I will kill her children with death, and all the churches shall know that I am He who searches the minds and hearts. And I will give each one of you according to your works."*

The Lord was speaking to John about the churches that existed during that timeframe but this is also representative of the churches of today – and He is very firm with churches that allow someone with the Jezebel spirit to operate and teach in the church and hurt other people by twisting scriptures and trying to gain more control and power over people while not being pure before the Lord. Jezebel knows which pastors will protect them due to their kindred spirits of like kind protecting each other and which ones to stay away from who discern something is not right inside of them. Jezebels are extremely perceptive and will try to "get in good" with the top leadership of their church or a ministry that will protect them so they have an advocate who will allow them to continue to operate. Most pastors are not equipped on how to address a person with the spirit of Jezebel, especially a physically attractive female Jezebel that knows how to touch their arms and shoulders and hug and play the victim role with an Academy award performance. It is important to have compassion for the person but vigilance against the evil of that wicked spirit. Separate the person from the evil spirit and if you are a pastor and do not know how to handle a person with this spirit then send them to a person who has had success in delivering people from

Jezebel or have them read this book and let the Holy Spirit convict them gently. There are not very many that have experience with delivering people from Jezebel in a loving way because it is so deceptive and people do not know how to deal with it nor want to address it so it may take some time to find the right individual. I have personally had tremendous success around the world with delivering those with the spirit as I have true compassion for the person that has it because of the trauma they experienced as an innocent child. The Jezebel spirit is extremely wicked and evil and must go before they can live a life of restored freedom and be involved in any ministry. God wants His Bride to be pure and spotless, not a Jezebel at the wedding supper. Ephesians 5:27 NKJV 27 *"that He might present her to Himself a glorious church, not having spot or wrinkle or any such thing, but that she should be holy and without blemish."*

If a pastor has been made aware of a person operating in the Jezebel spirit that attends his/her church and he/she does nothing about it to address it and get the person delivered from the spirit or removed from ministry in the church until they are ready to be set free then they will be held accountable by the Lord as He takes it very, very seriously. Often times the person with the Jezebel spirit will become close friends with the senior leadership of a church or their family members in order to obtain protection so that they will believe them over their spouse and remain safe from discovery. Jezebel is very adept at lying and very convincing so most pastors will not be able to discern who is telling the truth. The victim spouse normally endures the abuse for a long time before finally sharing the extreme things that they have endured and then it is hard to imagine that the Jezebel spouse could have done such things because they look so nice and innocent and have gained advocates in the church. Usually the Jezebel spouse will have threatened their Ahab spouse that if they ever tell anyone what they did that they will surely receive even more retribution as Jezebel loves to intimidate and strike fear in their victims. It is truly a life of fear that their victim lives in although people that know them would never guess all the torment that they have had to endure. Jezebel is a great actress that is very hard to detect until confronted and will play the victim sympathy card better than anyone.

So often times the person with Jezebel will have the church leadership duped into believing them due to planting seeds of lies for sometimes months or years in advance so when their victim spouse finally speaks up for themselves or tells their spouse they must separate then the church leadership will side with the Jezebel spirited person and shun the innocent spouse which causes them to feel abused all over again by the very people that are supposed to protect them. You simply cannot love the Jezebel person to freedom from the spirit and ignore their issues and believe their lies – because all it will do is give them more authority to do more damage to more people within the church and their spouse and children. If Jezebel is allowed to continue to operate in the church then what happens is that the church will usually start to experience a lot of strife and confusion among the people as the Lord does not take lightly, a church that is promoting, protecting, and supporting Jezebels.

If you are a church that has many people that operate in the gift of prophecy then you are a target of Jezebel and must know how to spot it and how to eradicate it. If not properly dealt with it can eventually cause a church split as good Godly people start to sense what is going on is not right and leave the church and is some cases the church will die and no one will be left and they will be forced to sell. Jezebel must be confronted lovingly but firmly and not loved blindly and ignored and allowed to operate. Jezebel can only survive if people believe their lies. Once the truth is brought out into the open the spirit loses its control and power over that person and they will realize that the lies they have told have been exposed so they must acknowledge that they have an issue and deal with it. Only then will they admit that they are suffering from it and can then receive true freedom by commanding the spirit to go from their lives once and for all.

If the senior pastor of the church cannot tell who is telling the truth then they need to sit down with both parties and do a thorough investigation and background check to determine who is telling the truth. Ask questions such as how was their relationship with their father and mother, what was their father and mother's lives like when they grew up, how many times have they been divorced, and talk to those who have counseled with them previously to get some outside confirmations and do not take at face value what the Jezebel suspected person is saying. Jezebel is a master of lying and making themselves look innocent or like a victim which is very frustrating to the real victims of Jezebel. The pastor must obtain the truth in order to help get the Jezebel spouse held accountable and to get them truly delivered. A pastor and his/her leadership must discern who is telling the truth and do their homework and draw near to the Lord because they can lose the majority of their church within a year if they support people with Jezebel, embrace and protect them as God will not be mocked and the Holy Spirit will stop flowing and more damage will be inflicted on the body of the church.

How can a pastor know who is telling the truth? In my experience if you look into both the husband and wife's eyes side by side you will be able to tell. The eyes of the lying Jezebel controlled person will look very anxious and nervous while the eyes of the victim look hopeless and exhausted and pleading for help. It is important to have them both in the room at the same time and not counsel them separately because the Jezebel person will be able to lie about everything without any correction from their spouse. If they are together and the victim shares about the truth of the abuse, their Jezebel spouse will often threaten to leave the room because they want to shut down the truth from being exposed about their behavior. They know how to manipulate the counselor or pastor in front of them and may even start to cry if they are a woman to gain the counselor's sympathy which brings disgust to their husband who was abused for years.

Women that have Jezebel are very hard to deal with if you are a male pastor or counselor because they really know how to get you to feel sorry for them and play a victim and have you give them sympathy. Usually the one that has been victimized by Jezebel will tell stories of abuse that may sound hard to believe but you will sense in your spirit they are being honest. Normally the abused victim will be able to come up with enough specific detailed abuse examples to cause the counselor to know they are not lying as the Jezebel spouse will not be able to cover all their tracks. If you still cannot tell who is telling the truth within a few months of time the real fruit of each person's spirits will eventually become evident. If the Jezebel person was doing a ministry it will no longer be flowing in the Holy Spirit and will usually be slowed or completely shut down by the Lord. The true innocent Godly person will see the Lord's hand in their life even greater and if they are in ministry it will be blessed and grow as the Lord will show people who was pure and blameless before Him. It will be evident to anyone that has just a semblance of discernment ability.

The spirit of Jezebel is the number one reason for divorce in the world today and also for dissension and church splits and collapses. People that deny the very existence of the Jezebel spirit usually are the ones that host the spirit the strongest and are trying to protect themselves and others in the church that have it. The Lord will eventually uncover and reveal the truth to others and there could be a messy shake out of those operating in that spirit until the truth is totally revealed to all and the people are either delivered or removed from leadership and possibly the church. It is especially challenging when the leadership at a church have pastors and deacons that have the Jezebel spirit and the situation then becomes public.

So, if you are tired of living a life of torment, misery, strife and believe that you could very well have this spirit, then you must pray a prayer of repentance and renunciation and truly take ownership of it in your heart. When you are done reading the prayer, Jezebel will usually depart immediately from you and you will feel a tremendous peace. You will feel lighter as the dark, oppressiveness of the spirit will depart for the first time in your life, but only if you are sincere and truly mean it with all your heart. If you are praying the prayers and then later say "I didn't really have the Jezebel spirit" or "The Holy Spirit told me that I did not have the Jezebel spirit" then you will not be delivered and will continue to suffer and your circumstances will become worse as the Lord will be forced to "up the ante" with you until you give the spirit up. If you truly mean it and the spirit leaves, then you will also notice immediately that the voices you were accustomed to hearing from the enemy will no longer tell you to do things that are counter to the Holy Spirit, to be harmful or deceptive. After praying this prayer many people will accurately hear the voice of the Lord very clearly for the first time without interference from the enemy. You will feel like the weight of the world has been lifted off your shoulders as years of deceit will be removed.

No longer will you have to protect yourself and any untruths that you have spoken or keep looking over your shoulder to cover up lies and other bad behavior. You will be free to share the truth and not feel condemned. Your loved ones will immediately see a noticeable change in your facial countenance and your whole personality will become more pure and Godly. You will be able to truly laugh, smile, and feel the love, peace, and joy of Christ for the first time. Your marriage will improve immediately and the need for continued marriage counseling will end as you begin to treat your spouse with love and respect. It is a beautiful thing to witness as I have seen this play out over and over again. Being delivered and set free is such a renewing experience for both spouses to experience!

Warning! You must be truly repentant in your heart and not just say the prayers of deliverance in order to appease your spouse just so you can live at home together with them and act good for a few days before returning to your domination and control. So read the prayers of deliverance and truly mean them with all your heart and watch what the Holy Spirit does for you. You will be amazed!

CHAPTER 7

THE PRAYERS TO FREEDOM

Make sure you are in a quiet place and have an attitude of seriousness, sincerity and contriteness in your heart before reading the following powerful renunciation prayers. Say this as if you can feel the spirit inside of you (and many will be able to feel it try to resist leaving) and you are taking back control of your life from Jezebel and Satan. Many will notice that right before you read these prayers that you will feel a presence trying to stop you from reading them as you may feel constrictions in your chest and your throat and voice and some have felt nauseous. Be aware that you may have several phone calls, texts and other interruptions that arise trying to keep you from reading these powerful prayers and being totally delivered. It has been my experience that those that refuse to read it have the Jezebel spirit at a strong level because they will deny they have it or that it even exists and thus will not get delivered from it as it will have a right to stay within the person and they will begin to suffer more in their life because now they have been made aware that they do have Jezebel and will not give it up. Remember that the Jezebel spirit is just an all-encompassing name for the spirits of control, manipulation, deceit, pride, anger, and exemplifies the evil woman that portrayed them. Those that think they may have it will read it easily and be completely set free instantly and feel amazing. There is no down side to reading these prayers….if you might have just a small influence of it in your life…you do not want to keep it! You need to read the prayers but you must be sincere with all of your heart in order to get truly free.

If you do have the spirit of Jezebel and you do not read the prayers to be delivered, then you will begin to have many negative circumstances continue to worsen from all sides of life. You may be afflicted with sickness and diseases that will not be healed because the spirit is present in you and the Lord wants it out. Remember what it says in Revelation 2:21-22 NKJV [21]*"And I gave her time to repent of her sexual immorality, and she did not repent. [22]Indeed I will cast her into a sickbed, and those who commit adultery with her into great tribulation, unless they repent of their deeds."*

Once you start reading these prayers you will notice that your body will feel less tense and more at peace as you take back what the enemy has stolen from you. Some of the petitioners that read these prayers may feel a stronger physical manifestation of the demons trying to stop them from reading it. It may become harder to breathe, they may feel strangled or some may even feel like gagging or yawn frequently. That is a sure sign you know that those spirits are present and do not want you to get freedom but instead want you to give up and let them stay until your death. Now be more determined than ever to take back your life from captivity. Make sure to read these prayers out loud as you take your authority in the spirit over the enemy. I will have you start with breaking off all generational curses, then move into the Jezebel prayer. I have also included the Ahab prayer which is very important for those of you who are married to or in relationship with a Jezebel to help them to get back the proper authority in Christ that they should have. I wrote a book for those struggling with the Ahab spirit called *Waking The Lion Within : Reclaiming Your Position In Christ* that would be excellent to read for those struggling with taking their authority in Christ spiritually. Lastly, pray the twisted spirit of Leviathan prayer. Are you ready? Go!

PRAYER TO BREAK OFF GENERATIONAL CURSES

I break all curses or vows that have ever been spoken over me from my mother and father and from all generational curses that have been spoken over anyone in my ancestry all the way back to Adam and Eve.

In Jesus Christ's name I declare that I am not in agreement with any form of sin, or disobedience that operates in this world and against the throne of God, as I am not in agreement to any person, or family member who deliberately sinned, or perverted God's ways. In the Mighty name of Jesus Christ I thank You Father God for Your good and righteous ways and I seek to live my life by Your Spirit and reap the rewards of living by Your righteousness.

I repent for every relative connected to my family ancestry who has deliberately, or without spiritual wisdom sinned against my Lord, or His people. I realize that all sin will be judged one day and that each one of us is accountable for what we have said, or done, but I am repenting for my families sins in that I shall be released from any curse these sins may have produced against me. I put all of my sins and my ancestors' sins at the foot of the cross and declare that Jesus Christ has paid the price and that Father God you have forgiven us for all.

I break all generational curses of pride, lust, perversion, rebellion, witchcraft, occult activity, idolatry, poverty, sickness, infirmity, disease, rejection, fear, confusion, addiction, death, and destruction in the name and by the blood of Jesus.

I curse all traumas in my ancestors and descendants lives that have had any right to me and command all memory of these to be forever forgotten and never remembered again. I replace these traumas with peace. I speak that any and all nightmares in sleep will be turned to joy and loving dreams and visions from the Lord.

I renounce the behavior of any relative in our family background who has lived more for the world, than for God. I renounce any ungodly beliefs, traditions, rituals, or customs that my people may have followed or acted upon. I repent of those family members who sought to fulfill the selfishness of their desires, and those who have perverted God's righteousness for I myself choose to serve God and live by His ways.

I declare that my descendants will receive blessing and favor from this day forward. That we will be blessed with love, joy and peace throughout our lives and that Jesus will be the King of our lives. I declare life and health to me and all in my family line in Jesus mighty name!

Amen.

Prayer to Renounce the Jezebel Spirit

Heavenly Father,

I come before you with a contrite, humble, and sincere heart. Thank you for having my eyes opened and scales removed today to the truth of what I have been battling in my life. I was truly a victim of my circumstances as I was an innocent child that was being controlled, manipulated and hurt through my father (and/or mother) as they were hurt by the enemy through their parents as did their ancestors as the pain and abuse was a vicious cycle that will now be broken over my life and all of my descendants. I am ready for this controlling spirit to be broken off of my life once and for all. Today I take back what the enemy has stolen from me and I command all painful memories of my past to be removed forever, never to be remembered again. I forgive all that have hurt me in my past and break off all spirits of offense that I have taken. I choose to forgive my father for all that he did to hurt me. I choose to forgive my mother for all that she did to hurt me (and you should name anyone else that has hurt you as there is power and healing in forgiveness).

I cancel every negative, unscriptural word ever spoken over my life and all physical, emotional or sexual acts that have hurt me throughout my lifetime. I break the power of the spirits of confusion, fear, control, anger, deceit, pride, arrogance and manipulation and exchange all hurts and pains from my past to be taken by Jesus Christ and forever healed and replaced with His love, joy and peace for the remainder of my days on earth. I command all the effects from serving the spirit of Jezebel be broken off of me and my descendants forever.

I command every demonic influence of any name from the spirit of Jezebel to be broken off of my life and I truly repent for my serving of these spirits intentionally or inadvertently. I renounce all wrong associations that I've had which served the spirit of Jezebel. I repent for all those that I have hurt with my controlling behavior and declare that I will no longer serve the powers of witchcraft from this moment forward. I declare a divorce with the spirit of Jezebel. I want nothing to do with the wickedness of that spirit in my life and declare that I will serve only the one true and living God with all of my being.

All the wounds that Jesus took for me on the cross were sufficient for me to be healed forever and I exchange my broken heart for a new heart that is soft, gentle, loving, pure, and strong (symbolically pull a knife out of your old heart and replace your heart with a new one from your heavenly Papa who loves you unconditionally).

I declare that I will serve Jesus Christ and His Word with all of my heart from this moment forward. I declare I will not compromise my living to any standard below Christ's love, purity, and Holiness. Thank you, Jesus, for healing my broken heart forevermore and giving me a new life to serve you with.

In Jesus blessed name. Amen!

Next just rest and take several deep breaths with your new clean and pure heart and receive the peace from your loving Papa Father. You should feel the weight of the world lifted from your shoulders and feel a tremendous peace like you may have never felt before. There is power in your words and life and death is in the power of your tongue.

PRAYER TO RENOUNCE THE SPIRIT OF AHAB

Father in Heaven, I come to You in the name of Jesus Christ, my Savior and Lord. Father, it is my desire to see Your Kingdom come into my life and into my marriage (or future marriage) and my family in a new and powerful way. Right now I make a decision to forgive any and everyone who has had influence in my life to cause me to be less than the person of God You wanted me to be. Father, I forgive the following persons who have unfairly controlled me (name anyone who comes to mind).

I repent of operating in the Ahab spirit and ask You to forgive me. I now take back the authority and responsibility You have given to me that I relinquished to Jezebel. By the power that works in me according to Your strength and anointing, I will watch over and minister to my new husband or wife in Christ and my children. Father, I ask for wisdom and guidance as I do this.

In the Name of Jesus, I break every curse that has come upon me or been spoken over me and my family because of the influence of the Spirit of Jezebel within my husband or wife and any sins of ours or our ancestors. I command every evil spirit that has come in through curses that I or others have spoken over me to leave me. Go out of me, now, in the name of Jesus Christ! You must also loose my (husband or wife) and family. I say to you evil spirits, Go! I declare that I am bold in the Lord and command restoration of everything that the Spirit of Jezebel has done to hurt me. I am blessed and highly favored and am strong in the Lord and decree that my future life will be far greater than my former. As a believer in Jesus Christ I have been granted the same authority as Christ and declare divine health throughout every cell in my body. I have the mind of Christ! I will help others that I know to become free from every Spirit of Jezebel and Spirit of Ahab and decree that I will have a strong anointing over those spirits the rest of my life.

Thank You Father for deliverance and healing, now and in the days to come. I Praise Your Holy Name. Amen!

CHAPTER 8

TWISTING THE TRUTH

Another common spirit that is found afflicting those that are anointed is the Leviathan spirit. Usually those that have the Jezebel spirit will also have the Leviathan spirit operating in them and will need to be dealt with effectively. A combination of Jezebel and Leviathan are extremely difficult to dislodge because the afflicted person has to command them to go. If the person has been tormented with them for 20 or more years they will often have entrenched mindsets in place which become strongholds that will cause them to deny they have those spirits.

Leviathan is a very seductive spirit that sets out to deceive the person that has them. It will present itself as a form of protection but unfortunately it is a false security, and will do all it can to prevent you from trusting God fully and completely. The reason you cannot trust God completely is because you could not trust your earthly father completely (and/or mother). The last statement should set off a huge light bulb inside of you if you have never had revelation of this before. Leviathan is a controlling spirit that will encourage you to take control of all your circumstances, instead of trusting in God to take care of your situation. That is why it is extremely hard for people that suffer from it to have peace in their lives as people with this are some of the most anxious people in the world. You are unable to be a person at peace and have a strong faith that God will meet your needs because of all the fear that is present. Those that have this spirit may notice that when they try to read their Bible that they often will fall asleep or do not remember what they read. They will also have a hard time sleeping through the night (insomnia) and may have bad dreams. Pastors that suffer from this have a very hard time delegating responsibilities to others in their church because they do not trust anyone else. People who carry Leviathan will struggle with strong pride and some arrogance in thinking they know everything about everything. This is especially prevalent in pastors that have the spirit as they may tell their congregations things like "We are the epicenter of revival" or "We teach things here that no other churches around us have revelation about" and "We teach other pastors insight that are not as in tune with the Father." The people that attend their church start to become more prideful with them and it is a nasty spirit that the Lord does not tolerate and eventually will humble the pastor or leaders that take that arrogant attitude. Some that have this spirit like to exaggerate stories to others in order to look good or to appear spiritually prominent and knowledgeable about everything and receive unique insight from God that others do not. They also will twist the truth of how a situation occurred and never take the responsibility for something that went bad.

Lack of unconditional love and receiving much rejection from one's earthly father is an open door for the spirit of anxiety to enter because you never feel at peace in your life. The spirit of anxiety is under the control of the Leviathan spirit. The spirit of anxiety wraps itself around your spine in order to control your central nervous system. An over-active nervous system is the reason why your body becomes flooded with adrenaline during times of fear and you behave so aggressively at times. When a lack of love from one's father enters the equation, this sets you up for a lifetime of pain and heartache that is unbearable. Your life becomes centered on receiving approval and if you do not receive it you feel guilt, shame, and condemnation. You probably have suffered much rejection from others (spouses, managers at work, pastors, etc), and as a result you are constantly seeking approval from God and from others. You constantly strive in your life and circumstances never feeling at peace or rest. You strive to be perfect and are driven to succeed and accomplish what you desire at all costs. Perfectionism is also a spirit that is under the control of Leviathan. Physical manifestations of Leviathan are a sore neck and shoulder area, due to carrying tension in your body most of the time. Can also lead to Fibromyalgia or cancer if you are in your 40's or 50's.

Leviathan is the great imitator. This spirit uses scripture to distort and twist the truth as it knows the Word of God very well but misapplies them according to what it wants to accomplish (does that sound like anyone else we know?...Satan?). For example the spirit may have the person tell their spouse "You need to cover and protect your wife and not expose me" while the abuse and extreme control continue to make your life horrible. If you keep a daily journal your spouse may demand that you not record the details of their controlling behavior and abuse. It is also causes one to be pious and religious. Leviathan loves to keep you from reading your Bible (you may read it for short periods of time and try to read it for hours but you often will fall asleep or not understand and comprehend what you just read so you try to read it again and again but still cannot remember or comprehend it). This spirit will prevent you from fully receiving the Word into your spirit as much as possible or will cause you to twist scripture. One misled pastor stated that God loves us so much that if you end up in hell that he will not allow you to suffer forever and burn in the lake of fire as He will take you out of the fire and put you some other place that is not as bad. Or that God loves you so much that he will just burn you completely up so you will not have to suffer anymore. This is very dangerous teaching that will cause people to believe that sin is not so bad and God is tolerant of sin. This will ultimately draw them away from a life of purity and righteousness to a life of sin away from the Lord. Never confuse God's unconditional love for your actions that are contrary to His will. God is a just God and although He wants no one to perish, if you choose to sin and want nothing to do with Him, then you will suffer tragic consequences on earth and eternally in hell.

Other pastors have taught that Jezebel was just an evil woman from the Old Testament and that the Jezebel talked about by John in Revelation was referring to an actual person in a church at Thyatira and the Lord was not symbolizing the situation for anyone in today's church. They teach there was no such thing as a spirit of Jezebel and not to worry. Why would that reference be listed in Revelation if that was not representative of today's church as each of the seven churches mentioned are representative of today's church? And how many women (and some men) have controlling spirits and are treating their spouses and others in the church with manipulation, lies, and deceit? And why would another woman named Jezebel be listed in the new testament of Revelation that sounds strangely similar to the first Jezebel listed in 1 Kings if the spirit is not active and well? Leviathan is good at teaching things that will hurt God's people and cause them to allow spirits to operate in them in order to protect the kindred spirits in others.

Other behaviors that one can notice if Leviathan is present are impatience and running ahead of God. This can be due to over-excitement, lack of patience, lack of Godly wisdom and even desiring spiritual prominence. The Bible tells us to be zealous, but unfortunately one can be overzealous. This overzealousness is one of the major strongholds of the Leviathan spirit that God wants to deliver us from. He wants us to be at peace and under control, not doing a hundred things at once with constant failures in ministry and confusion.

Your flesh can be over-excited and driving many of your behaviors. Instead of using God's wisdom and timing to reveal the revelations He gives to you, you are careless, immature and want it in your timing. Patience is not a word that describes someone that is being influenced by the spirit of Leviathan. You want it your way and you want it now. Instead of producing fruit, these revelations cause people to become wary and cautious of you because they were not ready to 'hear' what God was saying. Your heart has always been to help others, but you are also very much aware that there is an element within you that desires self-recognition and the spot light. This was the result of wounds of inferiority and lack of self-worth. Not only would you seek to glorify God, but you had a secret desire to glorify self too. It is important that you repent to God for viewing His glory and His works in an idolatrous way. You put your need for these things ahead of God when we really should be content with simply being with and knowing God. You may pray regularly to God for manifestations of His presence lest you become bored. Manifestations of His presence should always be for His glory, not our own selfish desires.

They will also suffer from false humility and self-righteousness; always telling others just how much they have had to go through in their lives and to get people to feel sorry for the cross that they have had to bear. They will exhibit behaviors to appear as if they are always giving their time to "help" others when in reality they are trying to get people to praise them for doing things for others. They will never do anything without wanting recognition from others. Think of them like modern day Pharisees who will do good things for others but only if those that know them are aware of it so they actually get praise and adulation from them. *They are like whitewashed tombs which indeed appear beautiful outwardly, but inside are full of dead men's bones and all uncleanness.*

They also try to justify their actions and convince people that they are right. Usually this is a result of an inferiority complex. Judging and having a critical spirit is another trait of those who carry this spirit. Discord and contention will be prevalent and confusion and mind blocking is a major attack of Leviathan. It brings in a spirit of distortion that will twist words so that you will hear differently than what people are actually saying. For example, if someone tells you that you look nice today, you will 'hear' sarcasm and believe they are really telling you that you look terrible. Or if someone asks if you need help you will twist it and take it personally that they think you are dumb and do not know what you are doing. Leviathan desires to divide and cause conflict and contention constantly.

The Leviathan spirit can afflict generations within the same family, especially if the father, grandfathers, great grandfathers or earlier ancestry on either the mother or father's side was involved in the Blue Lodge, Freemasons, Scottish Rite or York Rite, and Shriners. Members of those organizations pledge secret oaths to Allah and against Christianity. This dates back to the early 1700's in London, England and if members ever shared what went on in their meetings they pledge that a knife be poked in their eyes. Historically

Freemasons were known for their secrecy and a way to obtain more business contacts and thus become more financially successful. Many policemen, government, banking and other business related men looking for connections were common members. Those that are members today say to people outside of the organization that things are different than they used to be in the past but are they really?

Over the years, some people have claimed that Freemasons worship Lucifer, or Satan. The truth of the matter is that the name Lucifer is not found in the rituals of the Blue Lodge, or the York Rite. It is not apparent that Lucifer is mentioned by name in the Scottish Rite degrees, either. However, one of the "Sacred Words" in the 17th Degree of the Scottish Rite is "Abaddon," the angel of the bottomless pit, mentioned in Revelation 9:11 NKJV *"And they had as king over them the angel of the bottomless pit, whose name in Hebrew is Abaddon, but in Greek he has the name Apollyon."*

Worship does occur in Masonic Lodges. One of the primary purposes of Freemasonry is worship. Masons worship a god which they call the Great Architect of the Universe. The symbol they have chosen to represent their god is the All Seeing Eye, which the Egyptians used to represent their pagan god, Osiris. Many Masons are well aware of the pagan connection. It is clearly stated in a number of Masonic Monitors.

Since Freemasonry teaches a false plan of salvation, Masons are not following in the teachings of Jesus Christ. 2 John 1:9 NKJV says *"Whoever transgresses and does not abide in the doctrine of Christ does not have God. He who abides in the doctrine of Christ has both the Father and the Son."* So this allows us to know that since they are not following in the teachings of Jesus, they do not know God. Freemasonry is classic paganism. 1 Corinthians 10:20-21 NKJV states *[20] Rather, that the things which the Gentiles sacrifice they sacrifice to demons and not to God, and I do not want you to have fellowship with demons. [21] You cannot drink the cup of the Lord and the cup of demons; you cannot partake of the Lord's Table and of the table of demons."* This confirms that the sacrifices of pagans are offered to demons, rather than God. Although we can say with certainty that the god of Freemasonry is a demon, we do not know specifically which demon Masons worship in lodge. We simply know that they refer to their demon as the Great Architect of the Universe, or GAOTU. All demons are under the leadership of Satan. Therefore, Freemasons cannot avoid worshiping Satan by proxy. Very few of them realize the facts in this aspect of Masonic worship. A great many Masons, even some who do not claim to be Christians, would leave the lodge immediately if the names of Satan, or Lucifer, were substituted for the GAOTU in Masonic prayers. Satan would not allow that to occur, because the more effective lie is the one which is closer to the truth, without being true.

If an ancestor has ever been a Grandmaster of a lodge, or initiated into high level Witchcraft, the Leviathan spirit will increase into what is known as The Leviathan Curse. Persistent feelings of anxiety and neck or back pain are signs that one may be under *The Leviathan Curse*. You can, however, carry the Leviathan Spirit and not the curse. One woman was dying from 4th stage lung cancer and had a dream. In the dream was Jesus and her grandfather. Jesus told her that the reason she had cancer was because of her grandfather.

Leviathan is depicted as having seven heads which are Pride, A Critical Spirit, Confusion (Stupor), Impatience, A Lying tongue (Deception) and Contention (Discord, Hate, Murder). These are reflected in Proverbs 6:16-19: NKJV *"These six things the Lord hates, Yes, seven are an abomination to Him: A proud look, A lying tongue, Hands that shed innocent blood, A heart that devises wicked plans, Feet that are swift in running to evil, A false witness who speaks lies, And one who sows discord among brethren."*

Below is Job 41 which describes the Leviathan spirit:
New King James Version (NKJV)

*1 "Can you draw out Leviathan with a hook,
  Or snare his tongue with a line which you lower?*

*2 Can you put a reed through his nose,
  Or pierce his jaw with a hook?*

3 Will he make many supplications to you?
  Will he speak softly to you?

4 Will he make a covenant with you?
  Will you take him as a servant forever?

5 Will you play with him as with a bird,
  Or will you leash him for your maidens?

6 Will your companions make a banquet of him?
  Will they apportion him among the merchants?

7 Can you fill his skin with harpoons,
  Or his head with fishing spears?

8 Lay your hand on him;
  Remember the battle—
  Never do it again!

9 Indeed, any hope of overcoming him is false;
  Shall one not be overwhelmed at the sight of him?

10 No one is so fierce that he would dare stir him up.
  Who then is able to stand against Me?

11 Who has preceded Me, that I should pay him?
  Everything under heaven is Mine.

12 *"I will not conceal his limbs,*
   His mighty power, or his graceful proportions.

13 *Who can remove his outer coat?*
   Who can approach him with a double bridle?

14 *Who can open the doors of his face,*
   With his terrible teeth all around?

15 *His rows of scales are his pride,*
   Shut up tightly as with a seal;

16 *One is so near another*
   That no air can come between them;

17 *They are joined one to another,*
   They stick together and cannot be parted.

18 *His sneezings flash forth light,*
   And his eyes are like the eyelids of the morning.

19 *Out of his mouth go burning lights;*
   Sparks of fire shoot out.

20 *Smoke goes out of his nostrils,*
   As from a boiling pot and burning rushes.

21 *His breath kindles coals,*
   And a flame goes out of his mouth.

22 Strength dwells in his neck,
And sorrow dances before him.

23 The folds of his flesh are joined together;
They are firm on him and cannot be moved.

24 His heart is as hard as stone,
Even as hard as the lower millstone.

25 When he raises himself up, the mighty are afraid;
Because of his crashings they are beside themselves.

26 Though the sword reaches him, it cannot avail;
Nor does spear, dart, or javelin.

27 He regards iron as straw,
And bronze as rotten wood.

28 The arrow cannot make him flee;
Slingstones become like stubble to him.

29 Darts are regarded as straw;
He laughs at the threat of javelins.

30 His undersides are like sharp potsherds;
He spreads pointed marks in the mire.

31 He makes the deep boil like a pot;
He makes the sea like a pot of ointment.

32 He leaves a shining wake behind him;
* One would think the deep had white hair.*

33 On earth there is nothing like him,
* Which is made without fear.*

34 He beholds every high thing;
* He is king over all the children of pride.*

PRAYER TO RENOUNCE THE LEVIATHAN SPIRIT

Lord, I come before you with a humble and contrite spirit and command all spirits of pride to be gone from me forever in Jesus name. I ask you God to remove from my life any influence from the spirit of Leviathan. I reject this spirit completely with all my heart and command it to be broken off me forever, never to return. Forgive me for any ways that I have served this spirit either intentionally or inadvertently. Forgive me for any ways in which I have been twisted or have twisted the truth, that I have listened to distortion of the truth or have distorted the truth. I devote myself to bringing unity, not division or confusion, into the church and in my personal relationships and will therefore honor other Godly members and those you have placed in authority over me.

It states in Isaiah 27:1 *"In that day the Lord with His severe sword, great and strong, will punish Leviathan the fleeing serpent, Leviathan that twisted serpent; And He will slay the reptile that is in the sea"*. I declare that Leviathan is severed from my life now and forever more. By your grace I will speak the truth in love and dedicate myself to expressing the truth of your word in my life, and have a humble and contrite spirit in the precious name of Jesus. Amen."

I command Leviathan's head, body and tail be completely gone from my body and send you to hell in Jesus name! I declare that my back, discs and spine be completely aligned perfectly and any organs are untwisted and made perfect. I also speak to my legs that they are both the exact same length in Jesus name. All sickness and disease in my body be gone now and I declare every cell in my body be completely healed. Thank you Jesus!

THE SPIRIT OF ORION

Most pastors that operate under the influence of Jezebel and Leviathan will also suffer from the Spirit of Orion. Sally Atkinson does a great job of describing this spirit below:

Orion has been identified as the first lieutenant of Lucifer and will enter with any compromise of the Word of God. Under his control are many righteous counterfeits such as false peace, piety, prince charming and a great host of intellectual and philosophical spirits.

He is a very proud, beautiful, intelligent spirit and puts up a good front for a Christian or a church congregation. He will arrange false gifts to give a veneer of praise, worship, and spirituality, but genuine gifts will be hindered and limited. Beelzebub also works in the area of false gifts.

The demon delights in seizing ministers, particularly those in deliverance. He often demands that they make compromises in return for fame, glory, money, etc. For example, he may insist that ministry be confined to a specific area or only to certain people (cliques are common so only a few selected people can do what the pastor wants).

If forced out he will try to linger nearby, attempting to entangle victims. Pride is used as bait to undermine and infiltrate a ministry. Orion is especially interested in subverting deliverance ministries.

Orion will marshal family and peer pressures; semantic, philosophical, theological, and logical arguments against true ministry. These and other pressure tactics often lead to radical modifications or abandonment of the Biblical ministry of casting out evil spirits from people because we don't want to hurt anyone's feelings. They also will declare that Christians cannot have demons so that demons will continue to operate in Christians unabated.

Orion does not block all deliverance; he is much too shrewd for that. He allows ministry but sets firm limits. Once the victim is ensnared, the demon edits lifestyles, suppresses ministry, and makes workers complacent about true deliverance. Ministries start out with good intentions, but repeatedly end in failure due to the efforts of an Orion afflicted pastor.

If necessary, he will affect a physical move for workers from fruitful ministry to one devoid of the Lord's blessing. He will create and then supply all needs. He injects just enough guidance to cause the victim to believe he has heard from the Lord. Orion is quite capable of providing financial and physical blessings when it suits his ends. The one area which exposes these false situations is the absence of trust for spiritual guidance.

Be very careful if contemplating a move, checking and rechecking all with the Word and the Lord. Remember all of the past spiritual understandings which you know were bonafide. God does not alert you to a work He is beginning, only to pull you out without giving further understanding of His direction. Since God is not the author of confusion, be especially cautious if the move is created by pressure or lack.

In open confrontation with Orion, he will demand compromise in return for fame, honor and riches. He may insist on limitation of the area of your ministry or that he may be allowed to handpick those to whom you minister. More commonly, this sly spirit will gradually phase out any real deliverance or effectiveness in the ministry.

Be suspicious if your personality has not undergone serious changes as a result of your own deliverances. Beware if you still tend to be passive in your approach or have gone from an accelerated to a low speed life style. Orion will pull into play every yet undelivered area in your life to accomplish his task.

Orion favors the fair-haired, orator type personalities possessing a great deal of charisma which appeals to other people.

Although he favors men, he also preys on women who are very interested in spiritual things and have strong Jezebellian powers.

Orion concentrates on leaders and prefers those with education and natural beauty or social awareness and exposure. Controlling them will put him in a trusted position of authority over a body of believers.

When a dangerous demon gains entry, he influences through compromising of the Word; strong pride; and personal soul ties to a minister or acquaintance. To free a person from this influence – break the ungodly soul ties to anyone bound by Orion; then deal with pride (Leviathan); prince charming, Don Juan, charisma, attachment, witchcraft, psychic prayer and all spirits in charge of false gifts or false revelation.

Seek God and ferret out anything that would help to create an "I'm too good to be true" pastoral image. Also watch out for selfishness, self-centeredness, spiritual superiority, masculine superiority, the orator, rebellion, false ministry, and the false minister.

If forced out Orion always lingers nearby, attempting to reenter. He uses pride to undermine and infiltrate a ministry (pride goeth before destruction, Proverbs 16:18). He can enlist a type of perverted pride in the ability to be victorious over the enemy.

If you detect Orion seeking entry, first deal with pride and rebellion, then cut all ungodly soul ties. Next take a spiritual stand against all family and peer pressures, and all philosophical, semantic, theological and logical arguments against the deliverance ministry.

Warn the individual that Orion will continue his efforts. Special precautions should be taken never to compromise the Word, not to allow it to enter any area, especially concerning spiritual abilities or gifts.

To recap the behaviors that you will see with someone operating in the Spirit of Orion look for:

- Religious counterfeits
- False Teaching
- Compromise
- Charisma
- Pride
- Arrogance
- Evil fruit – false peace, piety, etc
- Mind control
- Witchcraft
- Self-centeredness
- Rebellion
- Rejection
- Lies and deceit
- Selfishness
- Philosophical arguments
- Theological twisting of the Word

PRAYER TO RENOUNCE THE ORION SPIRIT

Lord, I come before you with a humble and contrite spirit and ask that you forgive me for compromising your Word. Please forgive me for any and all false teachings that I have spoken and taught that have hurt your people. I ask you to remove from my life any influence from the spirit of Orion. I reject this spirit completely and with all my heart I command it to be broken off me forever, never to return. Forgive me for any ways that I have served this spirit either intentionally or inadvertently. Forgive me for any ways in which I have been twisted or have twisted the truth, that I have listened to distortion of the truth or have distorted the truth. Forgive me for my pride and thinking that I was above all others in my knowledge of the Word. I devote myself to bringing truth, not manipulation and a haughty spirit into the church and in my personal relationships and will therefore honor other Godly members and those you have placed in authority over me.

I declare that Orion is severed from my life now and forever more. By your grace I will speak the whole truth in love and dedicate myself to expressing the truth of your word in my life, and have a humble and contrite spirit in the precious name of Jesus. Amen.

CHAPTER 9

WHERE DO YOU GO FROM HERE?

Once you have commanded the spirits to go from you what is next? Many have told me that they feel tremendous peace, purity and humbleness as a weight lifted from their shoulders for the first time in their lives. Once they have read the prayers with intentional fervor to kick out the evil spirits, they receive healing and restoration. Many have also said that looking back they could honestly say that they were not really a true practicing Christian because of the voices they heard that were directing them to do things that were ungodly and hurtful to others. But now they can live in peace, love, and joy desperately desiring to make up to their spouse and children and others that they controlled and treated so poorly. Several have said that once delivered, they were able to look back and realize they were completely deceived and were very "me focused" and selfish while trying to appear loving and giving to others. They simply felt like a fake. They were like a Pharisee who wanted to appear like they were Godly, sweet, and kind to other people yet had a heart of deceit and evil that caused them great guilt and torment. Many also commented that they were fearful of trusting God in their lives and allowing their spouse or children to live in freedom. They were unable to give them unconditional love because they had never received it in childhood, and what you have never received, you cannot give to others.

Not all are delivered instantly. It has been my experience that those under the age of 30 tend to be delivered much more easily as the spirit has not had control of them for many years and the deep mindsets are not completely entrenched. Those between the ages of 30-40 often have more struggles to truly be 100% set free but their freedom also depends on just how harsh their parents treated them. The harsher the treatment the more challenging to become free will be. Those that are in their 40's and 50's and older tend to have a longer true deliverance process depending on how much physical pain and suffering they are currently experiencing. It could take many months or years to become totally set free. The spirits will not leave easily and continue to cause them to lie and deceive as they have mastered the art of deceit and given their minds over to the enemy.

The true barometer to judge your deliverance is your spouse and children because only they will know if you have truly changed and are now treating them with unconditional love and respect. You will be honest all of the time and love people like Christ loved and behave humble, without pride. The most significant sign is you will be able to be vulnerable, and have an open heart over an extended period of time. Some can fake it for a short time but not over several months if the spirits are still afflicting. Your pride and arrogance will come out because you cannot keep it concealed forever. If it has been 5-6 months of consistent humbleness in all attitudes and behaviors behind closed doors then the trust that your spouse and children had been waiting for will start to rebuild and hope will grow inside of their hearts that you sincerely are a changed person.

There will be little to compare in this world to the feeling when a victim of abuse for years and years can trust their former abuser for the first time. As their heart begins to open again and the love bond between them grows stronger than ever before due to the extreme former toxic nature of the relationship. What an amazing testimony you both will have! The victim will most likely cry tears of joy for several months depending how many years they received the controlling abuse. If your spouse senses that you do not love them the way that you should and there is still pride and arrogance being exhibited then you will know that the spirits are still controlling you and there will be a need to continue to battle to get total freedom.

Keep in mind that the Leviathan serpent is an extremely challenging foe as it states in Job 41 and that it has a tail that can continue to whip around and pull you back in with the spirit of pride and twisting of the truth. If you continue to try to influence your spouses' friends or tell them things to manipulate your spouse then you still have the spirits controlling you. If you act like you have changed but are not truly set free your spouse and children will know it and others that you are closest to may also see it. There may need to be a healthy time of separation from your spouse that needs to occur to have you gain complete freedom over the spirits afflicting you so that you no longer damage your spouse or children while you are working through complete freedom. Separation with the goal of reconciliation and not divorce should be the plan. I never advocate divorce as that is never the desire of the Lord.

If you have your prayer language I recommend praying in the spirit throughout the day as much as possible allowing your spirit-man to take control over your flesh and mind as when you pray in the spirit you are prophesying and declaring your future perfectly in the spirit so that your flesh will submit to the things of God.

Praying in tongues is a means of spiritual edification, or building up. The Bible says in 1 Corinthians 14:4 NKJV *"He who speaks in a tongue edifies himself, but he who prophesies edifies the church."* God is a spirit and when you pray in tongues, your spirit is in direct contact with God, who is a Spirit. When you pray in tongues you are talking to Him by divine, supernatural methods. Also when you pray in tongues it keeps you continually aware of the Holy Spirit's indwelling presence. If you are conscious of His indwelling presence of the Holy Spirit every day then that will affect the way you think, behave, and live.

Praying in tongues also eliminates the possibility of selfishness staying in our life. For example if you pray a prayer out of your own mind you may be praying something unscriptural or selfish. Just because I know how to pray does not mean that I pray as I should. Paul said in Romans 8:26 NKJV *"Likewise the Spirit also helps in our weaknesses. For we do not know what we should pray for as we ought, but the Spirit Himself makes intercession for us with groanings which cannot be uttered."* and the Message translation states *"Meanwhile, the moment we get tired in the waiting, God's Spirit is right alongside helping us along. If we don't know what to pray, it doesn't matter. He does our praying in and for us, making prayer out of our wordless sighs, our aching groans."*

The Holy Spirit is not going to do our praying for us. He is sent to help us pray. Speaking with other tongues is praying as the Spirit gives utterance. It is Spirit-directed praying and eliminates the possibility of selfishness in our prayers.

Praying in tongues helps you to learn to trust in God more fully. It builds one's faith to speak in tongues. Jude 20 NKJV says *"[20] But you, beloved, building yourselves up on your most holy faith, praying in the Holy Spirit, [21] keep yourselves in the love of God, looking for the mercy of our Lord Jesus Christ unto eternal life."*

Praying in tongues increases faith and helps us to learn how to trust God more completely. Faith must be exercised to speak with tongues because the Holy Spirit supernaturally directs the words we speak. Since we do not know what the next word will be we have to trust God for that and trusting God is one area of shortcoming that the person struggling to be free from Jezebel and Leviathan has.

James 3:8-10 NKJV says *"[8] But no man can tame the tongue. It is an unruly evil, full of deadly poison. [9] With it we bless our God and Father, and with it we curse men, who have been made in the similitude of God. [10] Out of the same mouth proceed blessing and cursing. My brethren, these things ought not to be so."*

Yielding your tongue to the Holy Spirit to speak with other tongues is a big step toward being able to fully yield all of your members to God for if you can control your tongue you can control any member of your body to God. That is a large part of the issue that has been affecting you - speaking out words of control and manipulation to your victims instead of being in love, joy and peace.

116

So as you can see when you pray more in the spirit you will naturally become more like Christ and more at peace.

Do things that bring you greater peace to your mind such as walking outside in nature on a path or around a lake or stream, riding a bike or listening to gentle praise and worship music. Take the time to feel the Lord's presence surround you. The more you can get away from other people and the usual day to day pressures and distractions of the world and alone with your Papa Father the better. He can speak to you more clearly and you can be better influenced by the perfect love of the Father instead of opinions from your friends.

Assuredly you never want unclean spirits afflicting your life again because they cause you to repel those that truly love you. If you have had many relationships that have broken up, you are unwilling to admit that it was you that caused brokenness as it is too much to bear the thought that the problem actually resided within you instead of them. The sooner you can admit that it was the enemy within you, the sooner the deliverance will occur, healing will begin, and true freedom will be the result. It really all boils down to this – do you trust God? Since your father (and/or mother) has hurt you so much it is extremely hard for you to trust and you have to be in control because no one else will protect you. That is a lie from the enemy that he has now ingrained a mindset that until you see and renounce, you will struggle with trusting God and therefore the enemy will have a right to control you. This in turn hurts your ability to trust those that love you.

God will protect you if you ask Him to show you in ways that you can understand. Your entire life you have lived in fear and insecurity, unable to trust in the Lord and it is time to give up your control completely and rely upon Him to protect and provide for you. It is like the commercials from the 1970's and 80's showing people taking the "Nestea plunge" where people would take a refreshing drink of tea and then fall backward into the swimming pool. You just need to fall backwards and trust that the Lord has got you because He does. The Lord is the perfect father that you never had and his arms are ready to wrap around you providing you comfort and security. You do not have to do it on your own anymore. You do not have to control all your circumstances in life. God's got this!

There is such freedom when you realize that God has it all under control and you can trust Him for all your needs. Psalms 33:4-5 NKJV *"⁴ For the word of the Lord is right, And all His work is done in truth. ⁵ He loves righteousness and justice; The earth is full of the goodness of the Lord."* Also Proverbs 3:5-6 NKJV *"⁵ Trust in the Lord with all your heart, And lean not on your own understanding; ⁶ In all your ways acknowledge Him, And He shall direct your paths."* And in the Message version it states for Proverbs 3:5-6 *"Trust God from the bottom of your heart; don't try to figure out everything on your own. Listen for God's voice in everything you do, everywhere you go; he's the one who will keep you on track."*

Morris Cerullo once called out a woman at one of his large conferences as the Lord spoke through him to her and said "Stop trying to figure things out!" There is a lot of truth to that statement. When we try to control everything then we are not trusting God for anything. We stress and strive so much in our lives because we were conditioned that way by our fathers (and/or mothers) who demanded us to live life according to their unhealthy standards. So to reprogram our mindsets takes time, to change from trusting in ourselves, to trusting totally in God. God most likely sent you a very gentle and loving spouse to love you (and perhaps 3 and 4 of them) but each time you caused them to leave you due to your controlling, manipulative, lying, deceptive, and abusive ways as you could not trust the Father and you lived out of fear. My heart bleeds for you because I cannot imagine what that must feel like to endure that much torment for a lifetime. Now is the time to finally say "enough is enough" and take back what the enemy has stolen from you and become completely free starting today.

John 8:34-36 NKJV says *"³⁴ Jesus answered them, "Most assuredly, I say to you, whoever commits sin is a slave of sin. ³⁵ "And a slave does not abide in the house forever, but a son abides forever. ³⁶ "Therefore if the Son makes you free, you shall be free indeed."*

In some cases when you just cannot get totally free after several months the Lord may lead you to go on a prolonged water only fast (of at least 14 days and even up to 40 days if the Lord directs) in order to sever completely the control those spirits have had over you for a lifetime.

The enemy wants to keep control of you for as long as he can because he knows once you are completely set free you will do major damage to him for the Kingdom of God. You will also help others that have suffered with these same spirits become delivered and set free. Many will deny that they have the Jezebel or Leviathan spirits or that they even exist in today's world. This torment could go on for months or even years until the circumstances become so challenging that it will become apparent God wants you to give up and command the spirits out. If it is obvious to your spouse and loved ones that you are exhibiting behavior that hurts them, then please do yourself a favor and take a step back and look at the situation from God's perspective in heaven. Look back at all of your relationships and see if there was any peace or true unconditional love being exhibited from you. I know it will be hard to imagine that you could have actually done something to have provoked them to frustration but if you are truly honest with yourself you will see a pattern. Pray that the scales from your eyes are removed so that you can see with the eyes of your spouse and children and of God.

Do you really want to suffer through one, two, three and even four or more divorces throughout your life? How many will it take before you see that you just may have a significant spiritual issue that is due to you and not the other person? I am not saying that everyone that has endured a divorce has the entire onus on them because in many cases a truly loving and meek person will marry a person with Jezebel and not be able to take the control and manipulation after many years and then leave them so they can have peace again. I am saying that in many of the cases of divorce there is one person who has been suffering with Jezebel and Leviathan spirits affecting them and until they have an "aha" moment of truth they will continue suffering. When they finally see what has been afflicting them from the beginning, as they have had many struggling and painful relationships, they will be changed forever as they now know what the root cause was and how to be healed. Jezebel simply cannot live in a peaceful loving state with anyone they are married to because they always have to command extreme control over their spouses because they live in a state of fear and anxiety and cannot trust. They will try to marry people that are meek that they can easily control but what kind of marriage is that – especially for the victim? It is pure misery. One man said his wife would not allow him to eat onions year after year and if he tried to eat them she would berate him until he gave up. Finally, after all of the extreme control of his life over many years took a toll on him, he left her and one of the first things he did was to eat some onion rings. He felt so amazingly free to no longer be berated just for eating something that brought him a little pleasure. Another man's wife would not allow him to have any friends come and visit nor could he and his wife ever spend time with other friends so that no one would learn the truth – for over 6 years. What kind of life and marriage is that?

Once you are truly free many have asked how you should treat your spouse, looking for ways to make up for all the pain that you caused them. My recommendation is to simply treat them like you would want to be treated – with unconditional love and respect - for the rest of your life. Your spouse will feel so elated that you are now treating them the way you should have always treated them and are no longer controlling them that you will really not need to do anything more than this. You may feel compelled to go out of your way to try to "make up for the past" but honestly your spouse will be glad that you are now set free and you can finally be at peace and no longer strive with them. They will feel so relieved and thankful to God that they can now live in harmony and peace with you and eventually you may start ministering to others that have these spirits and helping set them free. You will start hearing much more clearly from the Holy Spirit and you will no longer hear those voices of the enemy. You will probably want to make amends by letting others know the real truth about your spouse. And guess what – they will appreciate it and respect you much faster than you would have expected. Having honesty, integrity, and the true love of Christ with complete humbleness of heart is a beautiful thing. Also, going to counseling sessions every week and paying money yet never seeing the results you desired will be a thing of the past.

You should rest for a season after being completely delivered and enjoy your new life, marriage, and relationships and have fun. You will no longer feel driven, anxious, or fearful having to look over your shoulder in order to remember what lies you said to whom because it will all be truth. You and your spouse will have the greatest marriage you could have ever imagined. You will be able to rest in the love, peace and joy of the Holy Spirit. Your love for your spouse will feel amazing and free that you have never felt before. Philippians 4:6 states *"Be anxious for nothing, but in everything by prayer and supplication, with thanksgiving, let your requests be made known to God; and the peace of God, which surpasses all understanding, will guard your hearts and minds through Christ Jesus."*

Being restored to freedom in life is God's desire for you. It is time to expose the enemy for what he is – a liar and deceiver. I love you and want you to be free in all areas of your life and to go forth to help others become free in their lives and relationships by making them aware of what you have learned. Pass this information on as you know more people that have this spirit now that you have been better informed about the wiles of the enemy. You can help save marriages all over the world and bring more to the knowledge of the Truth as we are living in the last days and Christ is looking for a bride that is pure and spotless before Him.

CHAPTER 10

WHAT SHOULD SPOUSES DO?

Spouses who are married to those with the Jezebel and Leviathan spirits have asked me what they should do while waiting for their spouse to be completely free from all influence of the enemy spirits. Some have suffered just a few years while others twenty or more years and it is very hard to continue to have faith that your spouse will ever be able to be delivered and changed to a more loving and normal state after enduring all the abuse for so long. If you are still living with your spouse it will be more difficult for you to live in peace because your Jezebel afflicted spouse will continue to speak out against you as they try to overcome the enemy in them and you are their number one target, having controlled you for many years. Try to continue to remind yourself that your spouse is not the enemy (although it sure feels like it when you have to endure every day with the onslaught of verbal attacks and sometimes physical and sexual abuse). The real enemy is the demonic spirits that are controlling your spouse causing them to behave as they do. So the true enemy is the Enemy.

Ephesians 6:12-13 NKJV says *"12 For we do not wrestle against flesh and blood, but against principalities, against powers, against the rulers of the darkness of this age, against spiritual hosts of wickedness in the heavenly places. 13 Therefore take up the whole armor of God, that you may be able to withstand in the evil day, and having done all, to stand."*

A scene that will resonate in your spirit is in the popular Christian movie *"The War Room"* as it depicts a man who has been saying vicious things to his wife and was thinking of divorcing her as he was starting to have an emotional relationship with another woman who was also pursuing him physically. He has a dream and in the dream his wife is in trouble and is crying out to be rescued. She is being attacked by a man wearing a hood and his face is partially hidden. As the man runs to help his wife from the attacker he pulls the man off of her and when the man in the hood turns around he sees that it is actually himself that is attacking her. The man is shocked to see that he was the one that was actually hurting his wife. It is a good representation of what it has felt like for a person that has been suffering with their loved one that has the Jezebel spirit. It allows the person with the Jezebel spirit to visually see that all their life they have been hurting their spouse(s) but until they can see for themselves what they have done and are doing to their victim it feels to their victim like they are literally "sleeping with the enemy" to mention the name of another movie. You need to try as best you can to understand that it is the enemy in them that is attacking you and not them. This can be very hard to imagine since that is all you have seen for many years.

If your circumstances are such that you have no choice but to live with your spouse while he/she is trying to get free from the spirits, it would be wise to live as separately in the home as possible due to their constant internal battle that may cause them to try to engage you in strife. Many spouses will come to the decision that it is best to separate for a season with the end goal of coming back together once the Jezebel spouse is completely free (and ONLY when they are completely free or else you will receive their wrath even stronger again).

So what should you do on a daily, weekly or monthly basis until your spouse is totally free? What should become your new normal during this time of separateness?

1. Guard your heart. As much as your heart has been stepped on and trampled and beaten up by the enemy within your spouse – remember that Christ died on the cross for all our sins including those that your spouse has committed against you. Take comfort in knowing that Jesus loves that you are trying to help your spouse get free and that you will be rewarded for your faithfulness. Try as best as you can to have Jesus temporarily replace your spouse to rely upon totally to meet all your needs including your heart. It will be hard because when you envision who your spouse will be after they have been set free you want to reach out and re-connect with them hoping that they have changed only to be disappointed that the spirit is still upon them. God will also give you dreams and visions of your future spouse to comfort and provide confirmation that your faith in believing for their deliverance will come to pass.

2. Declare out loud what you want to see and never doubt. Decree and prophesy words that you are believing for and that will give power to changing your circumstances. Life and death is in the power of your tongue. Words like:

   - I declare that (first name of spouse) is completely set free from all spirits that are attacking him/her.
   - (First name of spouse) has a sound mind in Christ and no weapon formed against them will prosper.
   - Greater is He that is in (first name of spouse) than he that is in the world
   - (First name of spouse) has defeated the enemy in all ways and every plan of the enemy will be exposed for the lie that it is.

- And if you are dealing with divorce proceedings state "(First and last name) and I are married and have NO arguments in our marriage as her/his eyes are opened to who the real enemy is.
- I bind and rebuke all enemy interference from (first name of spouse) and command the enemy to go back to hell.
- I cancel all the plans of the enemy including divorce in Jesus name.
- I command the scales from (first name of spouse) eyes to be removed and allow them to see the truth that the enemy is within them.
- (First name of spouse) and I will be married for life and serve together in ministry against the spirit of Jezebel and Leviathan.

3. Take time to draw closer to God each and every day you are apart. Spend time listening to Him speak to you in your quiet and prayer time and when you wake up in the middle of the night. Put on soothing soaking music to listen to and just feel His presence envelop you and keep you in peace.

4. It is healthy to have one or two individuals that can support you from an emotional perspective. Do NOT confide in single spouses of the opposite sex (or unhealthy married spouses of the opposite sex) as that could open a door to the enemy to pull you away from your Jezebel affected spouse and lead you into sin yourself. These people would best be of the same sex as you so that the enemy cannot tempt you. They should be people who are close to the Lord in their lives and can encourage you to stay married and wait for your spouse to change. They should be good listeners to hear your pain and provide good Godly counsel and it would be best if they were aware of the Jezebel spirit and knew what to expect from them so that when they do things to hurt you they can let you know that it is not them but rather the enemy within them.

5. Pray in the spirit (tongues) as much as you can as that prophesies and declares your future and God's perfect will for you and your spouse. It also takes your mind out of the situation and allows your spirit to take control and provides you with more peace. Pray for at least 30 minutes or more a day preferably in the morning as it gives you peace and comfort to stay with you throughout the rest of the day. It is impossible to be angry or depressed after you pray in the spirit for 30 minutes – just try it!

6. Be careful not to share your pain with everyone in the world but only to those that the Holy Spirit brings to you that are healthy. You may share the truth in love with them as they may have been told lies from your spouse or others and yes the spirit of Jezebel loses control of its victim when it can no longer hide in lies of abuse and secrecy. It is hard to "take it" and let others believe lies about you but the Lord will bring out the truth in time to most and the fruit of the spirit in your spouse's life and your life will become more evident to all eventually. It may take months or years for most to learn the truth but realize that God knows the truth no matter what your spouse may lie about. God is the only one that matters and He will have your back and support.

7. If you have not already done this make sure you speak out the words "I choose to forgive (first name of spouse) for (and you can either list out everything they did that hurt you severely or just say for everything). This will be very healthy and therapeutic for you to speak out as you will feel your heart start to heal instead of getting corroded with resentment, bitterness, hatred and anger. Pray for a new heart from the Lord to come in and replace the scarred heart that you have endured. Forgiving them does not excuse them for the sins they did to hurt you but rather frees you in order to heal and keep sickness and disease away from you. It can be hard not to want to hate them because of all the hundreds of mean things that they did or said to and about you – but forgive them so that God can forgive you. Matthew 6:14-15 NKJV *14 For if you forgive men their trespasses, your*

heavenly Father will also forgive you. ^{15} *But if you do not forgive men their trespasses, neither will your Father forgive your trespasses.*"

8. Some pastors that have spoken to your spouse may believe their lies over your truth (especially if your spouse is a woman and they are men) and this will be very hard for you to take because it will feel like you are receiving abuse all over again but this time from someone that is supposed to stand up for what is right and provide a Godly protection. In those cases make sure that you choose to forgive them as they know not what they do. Jezebel is very deceiving and a master liar and a woman is especially adept at getting a male pastor to fall for her lies and some pastors have limited discernment abilities and will believe a pretty "innocent looking" face as the woman who has Jezebel can seduce them to believe anything. It is important you harbor no root of bitterness in your heart towards the pastors or counselors. God will correct them and in some cases they may lose a significant portion of members from their church or other parts of their ministry until they repent for supporting the Jezebel spirited person and help confront and hold them accountable and deliver them. God has your back and will eventually correct the errors of their way.

9. Recognize that Jezebel takes full advantage of a person who wants to be reconciled before the spirit is removed. It is very challenging because you may want to love your spouse because you feel sorry for them even though they abused you. That only feeds Jezebel's controlling ways more so you really cannot open yourself up. So be wise as a serpent and yet gentle as a dove when dealing with a person who is trying to convince you they have changed until you know in your spirit that they have changed and you can see that their heart is humble and contrite and they have no pride left in them. God will continue to make their circumstances harder and more restricting in order to make them sincerely want to change and be free from those tormenting spirits of control. Be patient as it always takes longer than we want to wait.

10. Spend as much time as you can in peace. Go for walks or runs around lakes, rivers or streams, the beach and in the woods, trails, etc. There is something about God's beautiful nature that causes a person to feel more at peace and feel His love. Do things that you enjoy doing (perhaps drawing, painting, working out, doing crafts, resting, riding a bike, writing a book, etc.). Stay away from people that cause strife and draw near to the Lord and times of peace. Being alone may not be enjoyable for you, but enjoy the freedom that you have to do more things for the Lord without worrying about what you have to do to please your spouse while you are waiting. There is truth in what Paul says in 1 Corinthians 7:32-33 NKJV *"32 But I want you to be without care. He who is unmarried cares for the things of the Lord. 33 But he who is married cares about the things of the world – how he may please his wife."* When you get back together the love you both have for each other will be amazing because you both will remember all the lonely nights of sleeping by yourself instead of together. You will have your greatest marriage ever when reconciled.

11. Exercise and eat healthy. It is very important to keep your physical body in working order as much as you are able. If you worked out before you separated continue to do it and do not let the enemy tempt you to cocoon and eat doughnuts and potato chips and become depressed. If you did not work out before you separated then start doing it. You will feel so much better when your blood gets pumping and you have more energy. Eat fruits and vegetables and stay away from fatty and sugary foods as those will bring you down and make you feel blah. Listen to worship/praise music when you work out to feed your spirit and keep your body feeling strong and vibrant and you will feel more positive throughout the day and week.

12. When you do communicate with your spouse try to limit any conversation that they try to draw you into that will produce conflict or strife. Email may be the best medium for

communications during this time. 2 Timothy 2:24-26 NKJV *"And a servant of the Lord must not quarrel but be gentle to all, able to teach, patient, in humility correcting those who are in opposition, if God perhaps will grant them repentance, so that they may know the truth, and that they may come to their senses and escape the snare of the devil, having been taken captive by him to do his will."*

13. You should have a few healthy, Godly friends that are praying for you regularly for encouragement and support during this stressful time but these are more distant friends than the one or two that you are closest with. These friends need to be praying for you and your spouse and supporting you to stay married or re-married if the spouse went through with a divorce. They should not be friends that encourage divorce or that talk badly about your spouse in ways that would cause you to want to divorce them. They should speak life and not death. They should be more intercessory type of people than those you talk with closely every day.

14. Learn about why the person received the Jezebel spirit to truly understand that they were hurt by their circumstances and if you had grown up in their shoes you may have been just like them. Have compassion on them like Christ does. He genuinely feels sorry for them because they got to where they are due to the harshness of their father and/or mother and the lack of unconditional love; it is much like a bully at school. All bullies were hurt by one or both of their parents and are simply taking out their pain on others. It is a similar concept. Your spouse is not a bad person – they are abusing out of their pain and God can use you to heal them of their wounds. Hurting people hurt people while healthy people heal people. Yes it can be an extreme case of loving like Christ loved the church in laying of your life down for them but what an amazing testimony that you could have and what a witness they would be to share with hundreds or thousands of hurting people about what you did for them.

15. Keep your mind focused on seeing your spouse set free and do not think about any other person or potential future spouse. God wants you to help them be free and restore the original marriage that you wanted and perhaps were promised by the Lord. No you cannot change their free will but as long as you stay in the game with them, the greater chance of a miracle that you will be a part of and what an amazing testimony of love that others will see. Yes there is nothing worse than being married to someone who has the spirit of Jezebel and Leviathan but what if you are their only chance to be set free from it. If they have gone through 2 or 3 other divorces before you because those spouses would not put up with the abuse and you chose to stay with them and / or possibly separate from them with a desire to reconcile then you could be their only hope. If you turn them down they may never have another chance and they may continue to go through divorces every 2-3 years. Jim Valvano the coach of the miracle upset winning team from NC State that beat the overwhelming favored Houston Cougars in the 1983 NCAA Championship Game developed cancer and his mantra was "Don't give up. Don't ever give up!" That is the same mantra that I want you to take with your spouse. In the movie "Fireproof" Kirk Cameron states "You never leave your partner! Especially in a fire!" – now that does not mean you cannot separate in order to get some peace from the enemy within your spouse – but it does mean you should not divorce without doing the things in this book to give them a chance to see the enemy within themselves so they have a last chance to be freed. I have had many people who were divorced from their spouses that said if they could get their Jezebelled spouse delivered that they would be interested in getting back together and re-marrying. Amen!

16. Love them like Christ loved the church but from a distance. Pray for them, intercede every day for them. Christ laid his life down for us and we are called to do the same. Sacrificial love is exactly that – giving up what we want for someone else and loving them. God never intended any of us to ever divorce and it hurts and grieves many people (including our

children) when we go through with it. Let the Holy Spirit convict your spouse through the situation and believe that they will make the changes needed. Speak out "(Your spouse's first name) and I will be married for life and live in peace, harmony and serve in ministry together to help others who are suffering to gain freedom." I wrote a book called *"Loving Like Christ : How To Love The Hard To Love People In Your Life"* that would be an excellent resource to read.

17. The enemy wants to discourage you by looking upon your circumstances but remember to continue to be like Abraham and call things that be not as though they were. Speak out what you want and stand on it. Keep your faith on, keep your love on and keep your peace on! Never let the enemy's voice penetrate you on what the Lord promised you.

18. Keep attending a good healthy Holy Spirit filled church. You may need to change churches from the one that you and your spouse attended together because they may have spoken lies to the leaders at their church about you and they will think that you were the "bad" one instead of the truth. So find a good healthy church and do NOT go looking for another spouse while you are waiting. Wear your wedding ring. Keep your faith on. If your spouse actually divorces you but you know the Lord has called you to wait for them to be convicted and changed then continue to wear your wedding ring because you did not divorce them – the enemy caused them to sin and divorce you. Wearing your ring will keep the enemy away from tempting those from the opposite sex to try to entice you and since you will be in a more challenged emotional state you will be an easy target. Do the right thing as unto the Lord.

19. What is love? Your spouse never knew what it was because they were never loved. Do you know what love really is? Let us turn to 1 Corinthians 13:4-13 NKJV

- ^{4} Love suffers long and is kind; love does not envy; love does not parade itself, is not puffed up;
- ^{5} does not behave rudely, does not seek its own, is not provoked, thinks no evil;
- ^{6} does not rejoice in iniquity, but rejoices in the truth;
- ^{7} bears all things, believes all things, hopes all things, endures all things.
- ^{8} Love never fails. But whether there are prophecies, they will fail; whether there are tongues, they will cease; whether there is knowledge, it will vanish away.
- ^{9} For we know in part and we prophesy in part.
- ^{10} But when that which is perfect has come, then that which is in part will be done away.
- ^{11} When I was a child, I spoke as a child, I understood as a child, I thought as a child; but when I became a man, I put away childish things.
- ^{12} For now we see in a mirror, dimly, but then face to face. Now I know in part, but then I shall know just as I also am known.
- ^{13} And now abide faith, hope, love, these three; but the greatest of these is love.

20. I love what the Message translation explains as to what love is as it becomes more clear ; 1 Corinthians 13:4-13 below:

- $^{4-7}$ Love never gives up.
- Love cares more for others than for self.
- Love doesn't want what it doesn't have.
- Love doesn't strut,
- Doesn't have a swelled head,
- Doesn't force itself on others,
- Isn't always "me first,"

- Doesn't fly off the handle,
- Doesn't keep score of the sins of others,
- Doesn't revel when others grovel,
- Takes pleasure in the flowering of truth,
- Puts up with anything,
- Trusts God always,
- Always looks for the best,
- Never looks back,
- But keeps going to the end.
- [8-10] Love never dies.
- Inspired speech will be over some day;
- praying in tongues will end;
- understanding will reach its limit.
- We know only a portion of the truth,
- and what we say about God is always incomplete.
- But when the Complete arrives, our incompletes will be canceled.
- [11] When I was an infant at my mother's breast, I gurgled and cooed like any infant. When I grew up, I left those infant ways for good.
- [12] We don't yet see things clearly. We're squinting in a fog, peering through a mist. But it won't be long before the weather clears and the sun shines bright! We'll see it all then, see it all as clearly as God sees us, knowing him directly just as he knows us!
- [13] But for right now, until that completeness, we have three things to do to lead us toward that consummation: Trust steadily in God, hope unswervingly, love extravagantly. And the best of the three is love.

There is no sugar coating this – dealing with a person who is trying to get free from the Jezebel and Leviathan spirits is extremely taxing and hard in every way imaginable. It is the most evil, wicked and deceptive spirit there is on earth and the hardest to get free from especially when it has become a stronghold in the mind for more than 25 years. What a testimony it will be to all that know you when your spouse is set completely free. Also watch what kind of dreams you have as the Lord will often times show you what your spouse will be like after they are delivered in order to give you hope not to give up on them before they are delivered. You will be able to see who they really are once they are set free from those spirits and it will bring tears to your eyes when you wake up. Your spouse that has the spirits will also have some dreams that show them who their spouse really is and how loving they really are and how they have contributed to the demise of their marriage and relationships. I know it is hard to stay the course and wait for your spouse to be delivered month after month and possibly more than a year but God will reward your faithfulness in many ways. It is very frustrating to have been abused for many years and then to continue to wait for your spouse to be delivered and set free especially if they divorced you and tried lying to people about you and blaming you for everything. It is an extreme example of loving someone like Christ loved the church.

If any of you have never read the Bible book of Hosea I would recommend it because it will resonate in your spirit. How could God possibly want you to suffer unjustly for another person? God told his obedient and faithful prophet Hosea to go out and find a wife. He then added the interesting instruction to Hosea that his wife was to be a prostitute (I am not saying that your Jezebel affected spouse was a prostitute so please do not confuse that with the intent of the story and its relation to someone that is married to a Jezebel suffering person but the sacrifice of loving someone who hurts you is very relevant). Hosea found a prostitute named Gomer with whom he fell in love. He then married her and they had children although not all of them were his as she had relations with other men.

Unfortunately Gomer found her life being a housewife and mother boring and she longed for the old days of excitement and living life by the seat of her pants. There were no thrills with her present life so she returned to the old one and began having relations with other men. Heartbroken, Hosea raised the children by himself and desperately missed the wife that he loved. After a period of time God returned to Hosea and told him to go out in search of Gomer to bring her back home. Hosea found his wife in all her wickedness and sin and bought her at an auction and then brought her back where he continued to love her and tend to her needs as she changed. God uses this peculiar story to illustrate the unfailing love that He has for His people. They, like Gomer, had turned their backs on God. They, like Gomer, proved themselves unfaithful to their commitment to God. With insignificance and willful intention they resumed their old lifestyle which did not honor God or obey his laws. Hosea mirrors the consistency of God's love for us just like we are called to do for our hurting spouse that treated us with disdain and every evil thing. Hosea 14:4 NKJV says *"I will heal their backsliding, I will love them freely, For My anger has turned away from him."*

Did Gomer deserve that kind of forgiveness? Do we? God's love extends beyond the limits of our sinful humanity. He longs to draw us into a state of restoration with himself. Just as He wants us to do for our spouse who is being controlled by Jezebel. However, merciful God that He is, adds this critical condition to His mercy in Hosea 5:15 NKJV *"15 I will return again to My place Till they acknowledge their offense. Then they will seek My face; In their affliction they will earnestly seek Me."*

So is there a line beyond which we dare not go because of our sin? Yes there is. Is there a line beyond which our spouse crosses because of their willingness to continue to abuse and control their spouse for years? Yes there is. The line is a refusal to acknowledge the sin, to confess that sin, and to ask for forgiveness for that sin. However, once confession occurs, so too, does forgiveness. The question is how long do we wait for our spouse to confess? Is there a time limit from God on how long he waits for us to repent and change?

God's desire that we return to him, love him and serve him faithfully is beautiful as will it be when our spouse asks for our forgiveness. Once they are convicted by the Holy Spirit for their part, then our part is to forgive freely and see how the Lord will restore what the enemy meant for evil. So what should we do when the only communication we receive continues to be controlling, manipulative and deceiving and there is no indication of any repentant heart of owning of the sins? Should you continue to seek them out and plead with them to change and to love you the right way? What did God do with His people? He allowed them to suffer for the choices they made to choose sin over Him and was silent to them. He allowed them to receive the consequences for their sin until they finally had enough and were ready to change. That is the position we should take with our Jezebel influenced spouses. Give them to the Lord and let Him bring their circumstances to misery and cause them to finally want to confess, repent and change. Loving someone like Christ loved the church does not mean to let them abuse you forever. Eventually you say enough and then let God take it from there.

So what should you do when you have to have communication with your spouse? Keep in mind that when Jezebel has almost all control of your spouse that your best option is to keep a low profile and minimize your communication with them because it will be fruitless and create more frustration in your life as you will be dealing directly with that spirit on them. When they have that spirit on them strongly you will not be able to get through to the real person that your spouse is in Christ. So try to limit all communication with them and give them completely over to the Lord and the Holy Spirit to convict them little by little. Some have asked me how long should they stay waiting for their spouse or former spouse to change? I respond with having them ask the Holy Spirit for direction on this. If the Lord promised you and confirmed it through many trusted people from multiple ministries that your spouse and you would do a powerful ministry together (and your spouse would be delivered) then I would recommend you stay waiting until they get free whether it takes 6 months, 1 year or longer. If you have not received any confirmations from anyone else as to what your future ministry with them would be then you need to make that decision between you and God. There comes a point when the Lord will tell you that you have given them hundreds and thousands of chances to change and repent and then they simply will not give up those spirits. So then He will give you a sign to release you. I know that at some point it is not what you want nor God wants but we simply cannot override someone's free will to stay in sin with Jezebel and Leviathan forever or they will shut your life down into such a depression possible physical sickness that you must leave to save your life. Their lives will become more miserable and that grieves the Holy Spirit but when you have done all you can do then you must give them to the Lord and let Him deal with them.

You are grief stricken because you loved them but if they do not want to change and be free then they are allowed to keep the spirits as their choice. My motto to everyone is to divorce Jezebel and stay married not the other way around. We cannot make anyone stay married and neither can God but there comes a point in time when a person has been abused enough. When the enemy starts coming against your ability to do ministry for the Lord and tries to shut you completely down then you must separate and wait for them to change. If they will not change then it is decision time. Never look back thinking what could have been. Give it your all with no regret; it is always more than you think you could have given while waiting upon them to change.

I love you all and am praying for everyone to please recognize that it is not your fault and not your spouse's or parents faults....it is ALWAYS the enemy's fault that causes people to hurt us. Know who the real enemy is. It is time to break the vicious cycle in your families before it goes to another generation and causes more pain to your grandchildren and great grandchildren and all future generations.. Stay positive and keep your faith, hope, and love on! God will reward you for your faithfulness with a beautiful new marriage (and my hope is that it will be to the same person) as long as you can both withstand the plans of the enemy. Be sure to put on the whole armor of God, as we fight not against flesh and blood... Ephesians 6:11-12.

REFERENCES

https://heavenawaits.wordpress.com/the-roots-of-jezebel/
https://heavenawaits.wordpress.com/healing-for-jezebel/
http://truthinreality.com/2012/09/24/30-consistent-traits-of-the-jezebel-spirit/
http://www.christianconnection.co/index.php/healing-a-deliverance/demonic-spirits-exposed
http://www.identitynetwork.net/apps/articles/default.asp?articleid=21917&columnid
http://www.freedomdeliverance.org/GenerationalCursePrayer.htm
http://www.christianconnection.co/images/stories/Prayers_from_website.pdf
http://www.theforbiddenknowledge.com/hardtruth/symbols3_index.htm
https://www.biblegateway.com/resources/all-women-bible/Jezebel-No-1
http://prideisamonster-leviathan.com/13801.html
http://www.ephesians5-11.org/gllink.htm

Final Thoughts

The Lord has told me that everyone knows many in their lives that are suffering from these spirits which cause such division in a marriage, family, work environment and church. Please make your family and friends aware that they can break the control and misery of their lives but they need to know why they are behaving like they are, what they are dealing with, who the real enemy is and how to be free. The enemy is not you or your spouse – the enemy is demonic spirits causing you to behave in ways that are not Godly, nor loving, and especially not peaceful and contradictory to the true Holy Spirit.

There are millions and millions of people who have no idea they are operating with the Jezebel and Leviathan spirits. They are living miserable lives and causing misery to those that they should be loving. So how can you be wiser than a serpent and get your loved ones and friends to read this book? Many have mailed the book to them with no return address on the package from another city or larger city. Then when they receive the book in the mail they have no idea who it came from and when they start to read it they realize that it is a book about their own lives. Then as they read through it the Holy Spirit confirms to them gently exactly what is going on in them to cause all the relationship challenges and then they read the prayers and are delivered instantly and their lives are changed and marriages saved! This book is truly a revelation from the Lord and is intended for such a time as this. Jesus will be coming back for a pure and spotless bride and it is time to get all demonic oppression out of our lives before it is too late. As Jesus said to John, the gates of Hell will not prevail against His Church!

If you would like me to speak and minister at your church, seminar or conference you may contact me on my website. If the revelations in this book have helped you and changed your life or saved your marriage you may wish to make a tax deductible donation to Restored to Freedom at http://www.restoredtofreedom.com which will help continue to get the message out to people all over the world that there is hope and a way to gain total freedom in Jesus. Amen.

41293624R10081

Made in the USA
Middletown, DE
08 March 2017